ZOLTÁN KODÁLY
HIS LIFE IN PICTURES AND DOCUMENTS

LÁSZLÓ EŐSZE

ZOLTÁN KODÁLY

HIS LIFE IN PICTURES AND DOCUMENTS

Special Edition for the Kodály Centenary

CORVINA KIADÓ

Title of the original: KODÁLY ZOLTÁN élete képekben és dokumentumokban
Zeneműkiadó, Budapest, 1971

*The following persons have obliged us greatly in compiling this volume
by placing photographs and manuscripts at our disposal:*
Mrs. Zoltán Kodály,
Mrs. Károly Escher, Annie Fischer, Mrs. Sándor Györffy, Nándor Heltai, István Kecskeméti,
Dezső Keresztury, Gyula Kertész, Mrs. Rezső Kókai, Mrs. László Lajtha, Margit Lukács,
Márton Máriaföldy, Domonkos Moldován, Antal Molnár, Kálmán Nádasdy, István Raics,
Alfred Schlee, Bence Szabolcsi, Júlia Székely, Erzsébet Szőnyi, Emil Telmányi and Rudolf
Vigh.

Second revised and enlarged edition
Translated by Barna Balogh and Gyula Gulyás
Translation revised by John R. Thompson
Design by Klára Rudas
Photograph on the jacket by Gyula Kertész
© László Eősze, 1971
ISBN 963 13 1414 6

Printed in Hungary, 1982
Kossuth Printing House, Budapest

Hungarians have lived in Central Europe since the end of the ninth century. They often played a prominent role in world affairs, but in spite of the fact that they were always a nation of singers, the outside world remained in ignorance of their music for many years. In fact, they created works of art in plain song in unison, and thousands of traditional songs composed by anonymous poets and bards were preserved in the villages. These were rarely collected or published, and thus remained unknown not only to foreigners but to Hungarian city-dwellers as well.

Hungary has given the world but a few great composers. Of these, the most noted spent the greater part of their lives abroad; i.e. Valentinus Bakfark Pannonius (1507–1576) and Franz Liszt (1811–1886). Others, like Ferenc Erkel (1810–1893), never got beyond the borders of their own country. In the early part of this century the situation underwent a radical change, and with the appearance of Béla Bartók and Zoltán Kodály a new era set in. A genuine Hungarian art music was born and raised to an international level. To perform the work of non-existent predecessors, this task was the work of a lifetime for the two composers. It began with the collection and recording of the folksongs sung in the villages, continued with their arrangement, and became consummate with their embodiment in the compositions.

One may wonder whether this sequence was a logical necessity or was merely due to the individual propensities of the two composers. It was, however, neither Kodály nor Bartók, but the Spanish musicologist Eximeno, who established the principle, as far back as 1774, that the art music of each people should be based on its folk music. What he might have thought to be an original approach was, however, merely a registration of facts, since the principle had already been realized in the subtle, though essential changes occurring in Italian, French and German music. Nevertheless, for historical reasons, the change came much later in certain other countries, and it was not until the early decades of the present century that similar ideals were established; in England by Vaughan Williams, in Spain by de Falla, in Rumania by Enescu, in Russia by Stravinsky and in Hungary by Bartók and Kodály. It could not have been a mere coincidence that all these composers were born between 1872 and 1882; although of different ambitions, they all seem to have been chosen by history and driven towards the same goal. They may only have been instinctively conscious of their common task, but as soon as they were convinced of its inevitable necessity, they consciously undertook its accomplishment. For some it was only a transitory phase but others made it their life's work. Of the latter, perhaps none entered into it with such devotion as Kodály. He was the youngest of them, born on December 16th, 1882, in Kecskemét, Hungary. From the outset he was conscious of the tremendous amount of work ahead of him. In Hungary the Turkish occupation (1541–1697) and the incessant struggle for independence and national survival had retarded economic and cultural development. With the rise to power of the House of Habsburg began the long hegemony of German culture, which relegated national traditions to the village, thus building a barrier between the culture of the peasants and that of the ruling classes. It was in this way that an ancient and valuable store of folksongs survived in the country, whilst a pseudo-Hungarian art music, little influenced by it and of less musical value, developed in the towns. Composers such as Franz Liszt and Ferenc Erkel, who might have evolved new musical ideals, were thus practically unable to get into touch with the original Hungarian folksong, surrounded as they were with a popular art music which had been influenced by contemporary musical platitudes. Of this new popular music Bartók wrote: "Despite the fact that, with its exotic character, it had a positive effect on a great composer like Liszt, it does not qualify as a basis on which a great Hungarian national art can be built." ("The Development of Art Music in Hungary", *The Chesterian,* 1922, No. 20.) In the same article he mentions the discovery he had made with Kodály: "We found in the most ancient Hungarian peasant music what at last proved to be a suitable material for forming the basis of a higher Hungarian art music." In one of his American lectures he assessed this material in the following words: "I am convinced that each of our original folk melodies is a practical paragon of consummate artistry of the highest order. In many ways, I regard these folksongs just as great works of art as, in the field of higher music, a fugue by Bach or a sonata by Mozart. Thus, apart from anything else, we may learn from this music an unparalleled terseness of expression, the elimination of everything that is unessential—and that was exactly what we were craving for after the diffuse loquacity of the romantic period." ("The Folksongs of Hungary", *Pro Musica,* 1928.)

In the same text Bartók said: "If I were asked to name the composer whose works are the most perfect embodiment of the Hungarian spirit, I would answer, Kodály. His work proves his faith in the Hungarian spirit. The obvious explanation is that all Kodály's composing activity is rooted only in Hungarian soil, but the deep inner reason is his unshakable faith and trust in the constructive power and future of his people."

Thus Bartók defines not only his colleague's stylistic trend but also his vocation.

Indeed, Kodály chose the harder way, for in contradiction to the ancient proverb, he wanted to be a prophet in his own country. As a composer, a musicologist and an educationalist, his only ambition was to serve his people. "With one hand I was a bard... with the other a teacher, an excavation worker, a bricklayer, a mason, a doctor... for I would have liked to have been everything that was ever needed," he said, in the preface to his collected writings. He served his people throughout his life. He did so because he was convinced that in this way he was serving mankind best. He deemed it his calling to recruit as large a following for high art at home as possible, and in the world, to rally even more supporters for Hungarian music.

His path was straight, and he spent his life in an endeavour to reach the goal he had recognized so early. His life was like a great and well-composed series of "variations" on a central theme; his compositions, his writings and his speeches had but one objective, the creation of a national music and culture. Arthur Bliss was right when he said in 1960: "The voice of Kodály in music is the voice of Hungary."

However, the way to recognition was by no means easy and his long career was an endless struggle. His enemies attacked him on just those qualities for which he was so admired by his followers. The nationalists called him destructive, because he accepted as authentic folk music only the songs of the lower social classes and ignored the popular art songs of the middle class. At the same time certain representatives of the *avant-garde* movement reproached him, for they regarded his works as second-hand interpretations and not individual compositions. Such criticism was, however, based on an ideological rather than an aesthetic evaluation, in the background of which lurked the struggle between different trends.

Folklorism or dodecaphony? That has been a controversial issue ever since the early 1920s. Like the antagonism that existed between German and Italian music throughout two hundred years earlier in musical history, it also gave rise to many debates. Kodály wrote in 1925, in an article entitled Hungarian Music: "In general, many people deny the significance of the folksong in the composition of higher music... Well, he who contends that the average European folksong is as a rule too primitive to have anything in common with higher art or with a more complex inner life, is right to some extent... Nevertheless, there are Hungarian melodies which for me and many others are an experience like that of a Beethoven theme. Let me add that an acquaintance with Hungarian folk music is far more important and fruitful for a Hungarian composer than their respective folksongs are for say German, French or Italian composers. In countries with old cultural traditions the basic substance of folk music had long before been absorbed in various forms of higher art. Great composers act as a huge collecting and retaining reservoir for the strength and emotions of their people. Bach condensed German folk music in such a way as had never been done by the composers of any other nation. German students of music who had absorbed Bach's compositions never had to devote so much attention to the study of folk music. The situation is quite different in this country. Our only tradition lies in folk music." On another occasion he declared with still more emphasis: "The Hungarian folksong is *par excellence* identical with Hungarian classical music. The evolution of Hungarian polyphonic music in the European sense could not have occurred in any other way." ("The Artistic Significance of the Hungarian Folksong", *Néptanítók Lapja*, 1929.)

These then were the roots, the purpose, the characteristics and the explanation of Kodály's folklorism. His life-work exemplifies the fusion of a missionary zeal with a historical necessity. He did what had to be done and could be done here in Hungary at that time, in the early part of the twentieth century. Like Bartók, he could never have become a zealous supporter of dodecaphony. The similar attitude adopted by these two composers proves that this could not be a mere chance; nor were their efforts the result of their individual inclinations. However, in this context Bartók said: "Though we have the same ideas about peasant music and its role in art music, there is a definite difference between us in our work. We both developed our respective individual styles, though we drew on common sources. And this was very fortunate because it could thus be proved that peasant music affords a great variety of possibilities in the composition of art music and that, though used as a starting point, it does not necessarily lead to the same results." ("Hungarian Music", *American Hungarian Observer*, June 4, 1944.)

It should be apparent by now that the German, French or Italian composers of this century could not possibly have set out on the road to folklorism in the way that Bartók and Kodály did: to do so would have been an anachronism. (As it would be today in Hungary, after Bartók and Kodály.) A folklorist Schoenberg or Webern is just as unthinkable as a Wagner who changed styles with Verdi. The composer must also adapt himself to the process of cultural development in his respective nation. Fully conscious of this fact Verdi wrote in one of his letters: "If Germans began with Bach and arrived at Wagner, they did good German work... But we who descend from Palestrina would be committing a musical sin, and doing useless and noxious work, if we were to imitate Bach." (To Franco Faccio, July 14, 1889.) And in another place: "If the artists and composers of the North and South follow diverse trends, it is all right, let them differ. Every one must preserve the specific characteristics of his nation..." (To Hans von Bülow, April 14, 1892.) On one occasion Wagner stated: "My artistic ideal stands or falls with Germany; my works live or die with her..." (A letter to the Bavarian King, Ludwig II, April 29, 1866.) Schoenberg himself admitted in one of his articles: "My music... springs from the traditions of German music... First of all Bach and Mozart were my teachers; and then Beethoven, Brahms and Wagner." (*National Music*, 1931; Josef Rufer: *Das Werk Arnold Schönbergs*, Kassel, 1959.)

Thus it can be seen that although music is generally accepted as an international language which asserts itself differently with different nations and in different periods, its national character cannot be neglected. In Bartók's opinion, "internationalism is unthinkable and detrimental to music as well as to all other arts. Music and other allied arts should at all times reflect the true character of their region and environment. Hence the great variety both in the arts and in life." ("The National Temperament in Music", *The Musical Times*, December 1, 1928.) Kodály also believed that "what is universally human can be approached by all peoples only through their specific, national characteristics". ("Zenei köznevelés" [Musical Education], published in 1945 in *Embernevelés*.) In this sense, he believed that the new Hungarian music belonged to universal culture, and he was against isolationism and one-sided orientation.

This was, however, only the main criterion of Kodály's art. No matter how deep were their roots in the songs of his people, his compositions can be linked with the great periods of musical history, Gregorian chants, Palestrina, Bach, both the classic and romantic masters and, most of all, with Debussy. The important role played by modal scales in his compositions is suggestive of the liturgical plain song of the Middle Ages. The contrapuntal interweaving of the choruses is akin to Palestrina's compositions. The block-like structure and Baroque idiom of his great choral works are reminiscent of Bach. The spirit of Viennese classicism can be felt in many of his works, testifying to an excellent sense of proportion and balance. Reminiscences of Brahms emerge here and there, mainly in the compositions of his student years. Debussy's music, which he discovered during a visit to Paris in 1907, was of vital importance to him: it enriched not only his world of harmony, but effected his entire musical thinking.

His art thus became a reservoir for the collection of many diverse influences. Kodály was a man striving for synthesis, and was able to bring together these diverse elements to form a musical unity. The *Psalmus Hungaricus,* the *Te Deum* and other similar works do not appear for one moment to be heterogeneous or eclectic compositions. And yet, a greater musical contrast can hardly be imagined than that between their various constituents, e.g. between the ancient pentatonic scales found in the folk music of eastern origin and the complicated range of harmonies in contemporary West-European art music. Nevertheless, all Kodály's compositions are original works, hewn from the same block. When he used colour effects borrowed from Debussy, he was always able to subject them to his individual melodic fantasy. And when employing traditional classical forms, he usually turned them into something new. It is characteristic of Kodály that he had a way of uniting contrasts. He shared the view of Frank Martin, who once said, "If there is anything worthwhile in art, it is its ability to unite elements that seemingly contradict each other." (Rudolf Klein: *Frank Martin,* Wien, 1960.)

From his early youth Kodály seems to have had an almost intrinsic duality in both his experiences and his studies. There are many apparently contradictory elements in this duality. Mozart's chamber music in the parental home, and his schoolmates' simple songs at the elementary school of Galánta, were in fact complementary, and influenced him simultaneously. Later, his first folksong collecting trips took place at the same time as his study tours to Bayreuth, Berlin and Paris. The fact that he was educated in the Hungarian countryside up to the age of eighteen, and only later moved to a Budapest still strongly influenced by German culture, was of decisive importance. Here he continued his studies, simultaneously, at the Academy of Music, the University and the Eötvös College of the University. He was awarded three degrees: as a composer in 1904, as a Hungarian-German teacher in 1905, and finally as a Doctor of Philosophy in 1906. Having prepared himself for both the career of an artist and that of a scholar, he entered the arena of life fully prepared. The theoretical knowledge that could be acquired from books, and the practical experience that could be gained through human endeavour shaped his diverse personality and his original artistic outlook.

These thorough and purposeful preparations may have been responsible for his success as a composer even in his early works. There is no trace of experimentation in his work, yet the fact that most of his first creative period was devoted to songs and chamber-pieces betrays a singular sense of responsibility. He seems to have refrained from undertaking anything that he felt might have been above him. He desired first to master the possibilities offered by the solo human voice and solo instrument before giving his musical message to the big ensemble or chorus.

He composed about fifty songs between 1905 and 1920. A few are arrangements of folksongs, but the vast majority are original compositions—the poems of contemporary and ancient poets set to music. It is characteristic of all of them that the line, form, dynamics, rhythm, and accompaniment of the melody are determined by the words. That is the reason why, to give just one example, *Late Melodies* (op. 6) and *Five Songs* (op. 9) are so different. In the former, composed in the spirit of the old masters, he adhered more to "classic-romantic" traditions whilst in the latter he gave a new voice to twentieth-century poetry. No single musician before Kodály had made such a detailed study of the rules of pronunciation and accentuation in speech. It was this knowledge that enabled him to set his Hungarian mother tongue to music and make it the perfect instrument of artistic expression. And since he was a composer with both vocal inspiration and poetic inclination, he became the creator of the new Hungarian art song.

The instrumental compositions of this period include piano works but concentrate mainly on string music. Some of the *Nine Piano Pieces* (op. 3) and the *Seven Piano Pieces* (op. 11) follow in the wake from French impressionism (e.g. the very impressive *Epitaph*) though most of them can be shown to have firm roots in folk music. The *Transylvanian Lament*, for example, is a wonderful example of a folksong arrangement. The influence of folk music is probably even stronger in the string chamber works, but at the same time Kodály's strict musical commitment helps rather than hinders him in the free unfolding of his individuality. In some of his compositions his adherence to folk music can be clearly seen, e.g. *First String Quartet* (op. 2), where a folksong is used as a motto in the opening theme, or *Sonata* for Cello and Piano (op. 4), with its opening pentatonic symbol. His source of inspiration is unmistakable even in the compositions in which he employed quite different methods. The *Duo* for Violin and 'Cello (op. 7) with its noble and deeply emotive pathos, the grandiose and virtuoso *Sonata* for Cello Solo (op. 8), or the *Second String Quartet* (op. 10) with its enthralling melodic invention, could not have been born anywhere else than on Hungarian soil. These works, and others such as the *Adagio* (1905), which became popular in several transcriptions, and the serene and clear *Serenade* for Two Violins and Viola (1919–20)—the opening and closing pieces of the "chamber-music period"—are the perpetuators of tradition, and yet they sound so new and original. They are the works of a composer who in his complexity created a totally individual and at the same time classical style which astonished audiences and provoked debate among music critics.

Kodály's chamber works were subsequently presented during the year 1910 in Budapest, Paris and Zurich. They were given a mixed reception. The audience was divided; there was an enthusiastic minority group but the majority protested. The range of melodies, whose roots were in the pentatonic scale, and the free, improvisation-like instrumental style were considered strange and unusual both here and abroad. Real Hungarian folk music was as little known in Hungary as it was abroad. Thus, while one Budapest critic considered the composer "consciously erratic", another acclaimed him because he "sought and found completely new concepts". There was one who blamed him for "despising thought and melody" and "avoiding harmony", and another who stated that Kodály "composes with a brilliantly modern, even an ultra-modern musical ability coupled with great musical erudition... yet his trend of thought is controlled with a Beethoven-like logic". In Paris the piano pieces of op. 3 created quite a storm: the "Koddalistes" and "Anti-Koddalistes" clashed over the works of this "young Barbarian". However, to be called a "Barbarian" was already a step towards recognition, because it separated Kodály from other over-refined and somewhat decadent trends, and highlighted the force of genuine, unspoiled folk music which radiated from his compositions.

Such a start held the promise of further success but Kodály's career was interrupted by the First World War. His new compositions would, in more favourable times, once again find a place in the musical life of the world. In 1921 Bartók made the following evaluation of Kodály's works from the chamber-music period: "The general characteristics of Kodály's compositions are melodic force, a full knowledge of form, and a slight inclination towards melancholy and doubt. He does not seek Dionysian ebriety but rather an inner contemplation, so there is not the slightest indication of a desire for the limelight. He is not readily accepted by the masses, but those who examine the internal, rather than external qualities of his music, will enjoy the humanity they find. And yet I must say it right now that Kodály's music is not the type of art which today would be called *modern:* it has nothing to do with the new atonal, bi-tonal or polytonal music. Everything is still based on the principle of tonal balance. Nevertheless, his language is new: he tells us things which have not yet been told, proving thereby that the tonal principle has still not lost its *raison d'être.*" ("On Modern Hungarian Music", *Il Pianoforte*, 1921.) The two years following his *Serenade,* 1921 and 1922, were silent so far as composition was concerned. He sent a few articles to various Austrian, French and Italian periodicals and spent the rest of his time with Bartók, preparing the edition of *Hungarian Folksongs from Transylvania.* We must come to know and understand this long silence just as well as we know his compositions if we wish to truly comprehend Kodály's individuality and artistic development. It deserves our attention all the more in that Kodály was then already forty, and at the peak of his creative power. Throughout his career this was the only break which distinctly separated two different creative periods. Before it, he had composed only songs and chamber-pieces, but after it—apart from a few exceptions—he composed anything but songs and chamber music. This negative symptom suggested that one of the characteristic features of the new period was to be an abundance in genre.

This pause led to a further development of his individuality, but as a matter of fact he could have attained this new period without an interruption in his activities. His silence cannot be satisfactorily explained by the changes that occurred in his circumstances, for it was just then that, after two years of rest—enforced on him for the role he played at the time of the Hungarian Republic of Councils (1919)—he resumed his post of professor at the Academy, and prepared several earlier compositions for his new publishers, Universal Edition of Vienna. All this would hardly have prevented him from proceeding on the road he had taken. And surveying his past activity could only have confirmed his previous conviction that folksongs must continue to be the source of his music and that he needed no change of style.

Yet, when he spoke again in 1923, he surprised the general public with a radical change. The *Psalmus Hungaricus* and the long series of compositions that followed made it apparent that during the silent period his art had become consummate in content and aim, though it had not changed in material or style. The decision to give his musical message to the orchestra instead of the solo instrument, and to the chorus instead of the solo voice, suggests a change in both his artistic and educational concepts. Chamber music had always been the genre of a chosen few, whereas Kodály sought contact with the general public. He wanted to bring art nearer to the people, and the people nearer to art. This demanded the renewal of his composing activity on one hand and the extension of his educational work on the other. At the beginning of this new period of missionary zeal he wrote the *Psalmus*. He continued to draw inspiration, as he had done before, from the people, but everything he received from the people he now returned—in compositions of a higher order—not only to a narrow circle but to all Hungarians.

The *Psalmus Hungaricus*, a work of staggering force for tenor solo, choir and orchestra, is one of the masterpieces of the twentieth century, an exalted manifestation of the union between a poet and his people. The words are by Mihály Vég, a sixteenth-century poet and preacher from Kecskemét; they are a free translation of King David's 55th Psalm. Kodály was captivated by the dramatic character, topicality, images and similes to be found in the words. After the hardships of the First World War and the subsequent revolution and counter-revolution, he justly sympathized with the words of the psalmist, who was persecuted by his enemies, as well as with the words of the Hungarian poet Mihály Vég, who lived under the depressing conditions of the Turkish occupation.

The content of the work may be divided into two parts. The first is the lamentation, the second, the invocation. As regards form it is a rondo with six interludes. The climax of Part One is the curse of the lonely poet [Bitter Death...]—the soloist's unaccompanied dissonant cry of pain in the awe-inspiring silence—and of Part Two, the prayer of the united people [You Lift up...]—the consonant hymn of the mixed choir with full orchestral accompaniment. These two symmetrically placed climaxes are in reversed values and not only hold and secure the stability of the structure, like two supporting pillars, but create the full harmony required by the content and form. The soft lauds of the introduction and conclusion form the lyric and epic framework of this dramatic fresco. Kodály renounces the solution, effective but wanton, of closing the work with the exalted chords of the second climax. Instead, he returns to the solid ground of reality, thus proclaiming the unity of life and art. After the success of the *Psalmus* in Budapest and Zurich, his next grandiose work, *The Adventures of Háry János* (1926), destined this time for the stage, was received with lively interest. Although Kodály did not create a modern, national form of opera with *Háry János*, or with the *Spinning Room* (1924–32) (lyrical scenes with folksongs from Transylvania), he did take a historical step: he presented the

Hungarian folksong in its original form for the first time in the Opera House. The melodies, mostly selected from his own collection, and scored either with a noble simplicity or else richly adorned, proved fit in both works for characterizing the various heroes and situations. Kodály's individual imagination, his ability to create atmosphere, and his descriptive or evocative strength assert themselves most freely in the orchestral pieces.

In *Háry János* historical fact and popular imagination are mixed. The hero himself was a soldier who actually lived, a veteran of the Napoleonic wars. To Kodály he was a symbol: "...Hungarian tale-telling imagination comes to life. Háry does not tell lies, he creates tales. Thus, he is like a poet. The story he tells never happened in reality, but since he lives what he relates, it must be truer than reality." ("Statement", *Magyar Színpad*, October 15–16, 1926.)

The music of this comic opera may be divided into two spheres. When presenting real life or Hungarian heroes Kodály uses folksong themes, when relating improbable adventures he composes merely to illustrate. The former is characterized by sincere lyricism and noble pathos, the latter by an irresistible humour and sarcastic mirth. The intellectual message of the work is contained in two very beautiful folksong arrangements: "This Side the Tisza, Beyond the Danube" is about true love, and "I'll Plough Up the Emperor's Courtyard" concerns true patriotism. These are the two main characteristics of the idealized portrait painted both of Háry and of the entire Hungarian peasantry. The orchestral "Intermezzo" and the "Recruiting Music" evoke the historical period. They conjure up and bring to life the soldierly *verbunkos* (recruiting music) style of former heroic times.

The contrast between the two different levels in the comic opera is still more conspicuous in the six-movement *Háry János Suite*. The odd-numbered movements evoke Háry's real background, and the even-numbered ones the amusing, naive characters and impossible adventures born of his imagination. Kodály is even more consistent as a true interpreter of his people with the *Spinning Room*. In this opera-sized popular ballad he employs only what the people sing even as his linking text. This composition is thus built of vocal and (mainly) choral parts. In the course of the quite simple story a motley picture unfolds with the aid of a multicoloured orchestra and many-voiced chorus, and presents the joys, sorrows, jokes, and triumphant optimism of life in a Transylvanian Székely village. The "Hungarian counterpoint", the simultaneous sounding of two folksongs, created by Kodály, blossoms out in all its splendour. The ensembles are characterized by imitative voice leading and a masterly handling of the choral texture.

The first independent symphonic composition of this period, the lyrical *Summer Evening* (1929–30), is the radical new revision, under Toscanini's inspiration, of one of Kodály's youthful compositions. Its musical material remains, but its interpretation is richer. In one of the variations of the many-sided themes, folksong elements and pentatonic phrases always come to the fore. The chamber-music instrumentation, which in the late-romantic atmosphere of the turn of the century was in definite opposition to the fashion in large ensembles, also remains in the *Summer Evening*. There are no trumpets, trombones, or percussion instruments, but the woodwind section plays a major role. The revision mostly affects the structure. The work, in its final form, is a sonata characterized by a perfect balance and a classical sense of proportion.

Summer Evening, a polyphonic composition, was followed by two homophonous works, *Dances of Marosszék* (1930) and *Dances from Galánta* (1933). Both of these symphonic dance poems were composed in the form of a rondo, though the build-up of the latter is less strict: the greater part of the work being made up of a four-section coda. The confrontation of the 'solo tutti' sections is another of their common characteristics. The musical material of both compositions has uncommon origins. The source of the first is old Transylvanian folk-dance music, and of the second, the music of the gypsies of Galánta at the end of the eighteenth century. As a result, the range of harmonies and the orchestration of the two works greatly differ. The character of the second is clearer and more brilliantly defined.

The two works composed by Kodály at the end of the 30s, *The Peacock* (1938–39) and *Concerto* (1939–40), present two different sides of his character. According to comparative folklorists, the melody of *The Peacock* has its roots in the most ancient pentatonic layer of Hungarian folk music. Exploiting the latent opportunities for variation in this folksong, Kodály avails himself of the almost unlimited possibilities offered by a modern orchestra, and creates a veritable apotheosis of the folksong. In his *Concerto*, on the other hand, true to its title, the Baroque principles of form and instrumentation reign supreme, whilst the melodic line of ancient folk music blends with the dancing rhythms of the newer Hungarian art music. In form, both works consist of three sections. The introduction to *The Peacock* forms an emotive unity with the first ten variations. The intermediate four variations are of a contrary character and play the role of a trio, while the last two along with the finale which is divided into three sections crown the work, developing further the giusto tune folk variation of the theme. In the *Concerto,* two quick dynamic movements flank a slow, lyric intermediate section. Moreover, the composition meets the requirements of the 'concerto grosso' style, and soloistic instrumentation, or rather the confrontation of smaller and greater groups is characteristic of the work. In contrast, each group of instruments is assigned a special task throughout the whole composition of *The Peacock*.

Despite the numerous and large-scale orchestral compositions completed during these years, they cannot be regarded as Kodály's "symphonic period" because his interest was more and more turned to vocal genres, especially to choruses. Prior to the *Psalmus,* about 50 songs and 6 choral works had been completed. After it the inverse was true: as against a hundred choral works only a few original songs appeared. The fifty-seven songs published in the ten volumes entitled *Hungarian Folk Music* are but folksong adaptations. He composed all kinds of choral works, but the compositions for children's choirs were nearest to his heart. What he created in this field is truly unique in the musical literature of the twentieth century. To give the reader an idea of Kodály's contribution in this field, let us refer to just a few musical events around that time:

On 2 April 1925, the boys' choir of a Budapest school performed Kodály's first children's choral works, the *Straw Guy* and *See, the Gypsy Munching Cheese*.

On 14 April 1929, seven hundred pupils from seven different schools performed thirteen of Kodály's children's choruses. (The concert had to be repeated twice.)

On 28 April 1934, one thousand five hundred pupils from fourteen schools gave a "Kodály Children's Chorus Evening". (The festival that gave the name to the movement "Singing Youth".)

In May 1935, in addition to Budapest, the young people of seven Hungarian country towns arranged singing festivals.

During a period of ten years there was a large increase in the number of choruses, chorus masters and choral works. This was Kodály's achievement, or rather the achievement of both Kodály and his followers. An explanation for this achievement can be found in the strength of his convictions. In an article he wrote: "No one is too great to compose for the young. Indeed, he must strive to be great enough for this. Original works should be composed, in which the words, the melody and the colour spring from the child's voice and the child's mind..." ("Children's Choruses", *Zenei Szemle*, 1929.) Of such compositions, *Lengyel László*, *Whitsuntide*, *The Swallow's Wooing*, *Dancing Song* and *Epiphany* are examples, though some fifty songs were completed in this series. These choruses appear to contain many of the complicated musical effects of part-song composition. They are, however, plain, and have relatively straightforward formal structure. What's more, each part is easy to sing and of the same standard. For their youthful singers the works are suggestive of the joys of creation for they radiate the very spirit of childhood-playing at 'life', and living through the play.

Kodály completed about twenty choral works for male voice and another twenty for female voice, such as the *Songs from Karád, The Ruins, The Peacock,* respectively the five songs without words, *Mountain Nights* and the *Four Italian Madrigals*. However, among his a cappella choruses, the place of honour is taken by those for mixed chorus. In Kodály's own opinion: "Works which proclaim the fullness of life also need the fullness of the human voice." ("Excelsior", *Magyar Dal*, 1937.) He began the series with the composition of *Mátra Pictures* in 1931. This large-scale folksong suite was composed in opposition to the German Liedertafel style and its alien spirit, and this helped to prepare the way for the reception of his later choral works by the public. Some of these, *The Aged, Too Late, Ode to Franz Liszt, Norwegian Girls,* and especially *Jesus and the Traders,* herald the renaissance of European choral literature. *Jesus and the Traders* is a fine example of Kodály's choral brilliance. Its structure is balanced; the brief and homophonic introduction and conclusion form the framework for a large-scale polyphonic movement which comprises three sections. The first is the exposition of the drama in which imitative techniques are used to introduce the traders and money-lenders. The second part, with its fugato-like opening, describes how they are chased from the temple, and provides the action. Part Three (the teaching) leads us, with a great heightening of emotion, to the climax. The naturalness with which the independent handling of the parts blends with the requirements of euphony originates from a synthesis of linear and vertical thinking. The resuscitation of the passions, only latent in the words and the multiplication of their strength, is the result of a rich creative imagination together with great professional skill.

The character, importance and length of the *Te Deum* (1936) written for solo quartet, mixed choir, organ and orchestra link it with the *Psalmus*, both in its high order of unity and in its artistic fullness. It is an exceedingly concentrated composition. One of its chief merits is that it is a well-balanced composition—in spite of the fact that in no other work did Kodály align so many different elements. The *Te Deum* has a very complex form, but its outline may be clearly understood for it is in the modern "bogen form", having symmetrically placed twin climaxes ("Pleni sunt" and "Non confundar"). The technical solution of the two fugato sections is reminiscent of Baroque choral polyphony, whereas the musical content is evocative of old Hungarian folksongs. In this culminating and comprehensive work Kodály thus connects ancient tradition with modern effects, popular art with high art, and Hungary with Europe. And in doing so again symbolically declares his adherence to the great synthesis.

The feverish activity of the last creative period—the twenty-six years from 1941 until his death in March 1967—extended to nearly all genres, with the exception of song and chamber music. In comparison with the previous period, two changes can be observed. On the one hand, the proportion of vocal compositions to instrumental compositions increased and on the other, educational works appeared with the booklets containing *Bicinia Hungarica, Fifteen Two-Part Excercises,* and *Let Us Sing Correctly!* The roots of these two changes are common: both spring from the strengthening of Kodály as an authority on cultural policy and as an educationalist.

However, even a precursory glance at the work completed during this period should convince us that this change did not occur to the detriment of the creative Kodály, for he composed *Missa Brevis* (1944), *Kálló Folk Dances* (1950), *Zrínyi's Appeal* (1955), *Symphony* (1961) and *Laudes Organi* (1966), to mention only some of the more outstanding pieces. The *Missa Brevis* crowns Kodály's church-music compositions and summarizes the valuable traditions of European church music from Gregorian music to Palestrina, Bach and the great Romantics. It was composed "tempore belli" (in time of war) and yet the overall effect of it is elevating with the final chorus radiating hope and raising the spirits of the despondent. *"Da pacem!"* he cries in the name of the suffering millions: *"Give us peace!"*

The *Kálló Folk Dances* evoke a gay and popular dance festival. The melodies were recorded by Kodály in 1937 at Nagykálló. The arrangement—composed for mixed chorus and folk orchestra—and style suit the historical origin of the music. In the first movement of this three-part work a lyrically soaring giusto dance-song is heard. This is followed by a bagpipe-like quicker movement. It closes—attacca—with a dynamic finale.

Zrínyi's Appeal, composed for baritone solo and mixed chorus, shows quite another world. The words, by Miklós Zrínyi, the seventeenth-century military leader and poet, are from one of his prose works. The music not only closely follows the rich imagery of the words but brings out their unspoken emotional content. The composition starts with a soft-voiced recitative and closes with the soaring jubilation of the choir. The middle section provides a vigorous development of the dramatic message and demonstrates all the virtues of Kodály's a cappella art.

The grandiose *Symphony* was the fruit of long years of preparation. The sequence of its movements and the thematic affinity of Movement I to III are suggestive of the three-section Italian *sinfonia.* The key (C major) demonstrates Kodály's attachment to the principle of strict tonality, and the introduction of the theme in unison several times shows his attachment to the leading role of the melody. The material of the theme has its roots in folksong, while the construction and form are based on pure classical traditions. The *Symphony* is at the same time a consummation and a glance backward. The work is the undertaking of a life which knew no compromise, a summary of earlier achievements and a declaration of faith in the ideals he had professed for decades.

The keystone of his uninterrupted artistic development is the last great work, *Laudes Organi,* composed for mixed chorus and organ. The ornate Latin text and the twelfth-century sequence came down to us through a contemporary codex. Kodály made use of these to create an elaborate piece. The plain melody is endowed with a rich harmonization abounding in modulations. The free form, resulting from the succession of chorus and organ, is crowned by a concise and final fugue of noble character. Kodály completed *Laudes Organi* at the age of eighty-four, yet there is no trace of any tiredness or exhaustion of creative inspiration in the composition. Seven decades had passed since his first attempts at composing and about six decades since his first mature composition. He had had a long career, absolutely lacking in changes of style or spectacular turns. His unbroken development can be followed from period to period. He was an artist who constantly renewed his sources of inspiration from his own roots. Two other branches of his activity were of help to him: his musicological research provided the main source of musical inspiration, while his educational activity increased the scope and the range of his art. Both of these activities are valuable enough to be examined separately in the present appreciation of Kodály. In an examination of Kodály's work in the field of folklore research we should cast a glance at the antecedents. In 1832 the Hungarian Learned Society (predecessor of the Hungarian Academy of Sciences) published for the first time an invitation to collect folksongs. As a result, ten collections were made. The words of the folksongs partly appeared in print fifteen years later, but with a few exceptions, the melodies were lost. In 1838 Franz Liszt, then twenty-seven years old, planned to go on a folksong collecting tour on foot, with a knapsack on his back. He wanted to visit Hungary's most secluded spots, but he never got as far as peasant cottages or huts, and in the homes of wealthy, eminent men he did not come across a single folksong.

In the first exchange of letters between the two great Hungarian poets Sándor Petőfi (1823–1849) and János Arany (1817–1882) can be seen the following references: "...Folk-poetry is the true poetry. Let us make it rule supreme", Petőfi wrote on 4 February 1847. "I cannot expect a national poetry before the blossoming of folk-poetry is achieved," Arany replied on 11 February. He later brought up the subject again in a criticism: "...Our folk music has already lost much of its original zest. Let us save what we can." ("Popular Tales of the West Highlands", ed. by J. F. Campbell, 1861.) The two great poets thus kept the idea awake, but the carrying out of the task had to wait for a musician. Some collections did appear in the next few decades, but those who edited them were either amateurs or were educated and influenced by foreign music. They discovered a thin layer of original folksongs but at the same time they distorted them, embellished them according to their own taste, or provided piano accompaniment in such a way that the original songs were completely falsified. Béla Vikár, a parliamentary stenographer, started collecting in the 1890s, with the most modern mechanical device of the period—Edison's phonograph. But he was unable to take down the tunes he had recorded because he was not a trained musician.

Unrealized plans and abortive attempts were characteristic of the situation at the turn of the century. Only in a few professional quarters was there any knowledge of these collections, and no one had any idea of their short-comings. During his years at college and university Kodály studied such collections. He recognized what had to be done and set to work immediately. He was not a pioneer in the strict sense of the word—indeed, no one appreciated more than he the activities of his predecessors—and yet he was the first researcher in Hungary whose high scientific and musical erudition and individual aspirations made him fit for such a tremendous task. He found a great comrade-in-arms in Béla Bartók, with whom he co-operated from 1906 to 1940. He was also helped by László Lajtha, Antal Molnár, and an increasingly numerous team of co-workers who had previously been his pupils.

His methods are revealed in the sequence of his publications. First a few selections of his own collection of folksongs were published. But twelve years went by before his first principled theoretical article came out ("The Pentatonic Scale in Hungarian Folk Music", 1917). The work of the following twenty years included publications which elaborated on certain related fields and provided material for his comprehensive monograph (*The Folk Music of Hungary*, 1937). He lived to see the gathering of the harvest —the first volumes of *A Magyar Népzene Tára [Corpus Musicae Popularis Hungaricae]*, arranged for the press by the Folk Music Research Group under his guidance: I. *Children's Games*, 1951, II. *Calendar Customs' Songs*, 1953, III. *Wedding Songs*, Part One 1955, Part Two 1956, IV. *Pairing Songs*, 1959, V. *Laments*, 1966.

Kodály's scientific activity is one tremendous crescendo. His guiding principle was: "A thorough knowledge of the material must precede everything, for everything else can be built only upon this knowledge. Any efforts to achieve aesthetic results which either precede or discard knowledge are equivalent to building castles in Spain." ("Three Hungarian Songs by Lukács Mihálovits", *Új Zenei Szemle,* 1951.) "Theories become antiquated but faultlessly published material never does," he added in the preface to his *Calendar Customs' Songs.* In recognition of his work many honorary degrees were conferred upon him, and he was elected an honorary member of several academies. The International Folk Music Council elected him President in 1961.

The activities of Kodály the scholar and Kodály the educationalist met at several points. As President of the Hungarian Academy of Sciences he emphasized that the Academy, "in addition to professional fields of research, must devote attention to the popularization of scientific study as well. This cannot be left to bunglers and pseudo-scholars. The best are just good enough for this purpose." ("*Presidential Address" at the General Assembly of the Hungarian Academy of Sciences* on 4 July 1948.) It was in this spirit that he worked at all times. When, from 1917 onwards, he was working as a music critic, he wanted not only to inform the reading public but also to educate it. It was at the same time in these articles that he laid the foundations for Bartókian aesthetics. In a similar way, Kodály the scholar supported Kodály the educationalist when he spoke of the importance of Hungarian folksongs, or when in 1937, he began a campaign for the correct pronunciation of the Hungarian language.

Sometimes it was the educationalist that came to the fore, at other times the scholar; depending on which was needed most. In the second half of his career the former played the leading role. The crescendo that can be observed in his musicological research activity became more and more obvious. At the outset he was engaged only in the training of musicians. From 1907 onwards he taught musical theory and later composition at the Liszt Ferenc Academy of Music. After realizing in 1925, that the youth "are brought up in complete musical depravity, which is worse than illiteracy", he spent more and more time on the emotional and aesthetic education of school-children. He created a whole series of choruses for children and provided them with singing and reading exercises. Finally, from the 30s onwards, he devoted his full attention to the chorus movement. He composed numerous works for all kinds of ensembles, and expounded his views in a series of essays, articles and lectures. As soon as he became aware of the interdependence of vocational training and audience education, he decided to endeavour for the rest of his life to try and achieve a balance between the two, and to bridge the ever widening gap between active and passive musicians. During the last part of his life he was virtually teaching the whole of Hungary how to sing. He wanted to give a musical education to his people and in doing so to make them happier.

He expressed his conviction that singing is more important than anything else, in an introductory article he wrote in 1941 for the periodical *Singing Youth.* "A deeper musical education can at all times develop only where singing forms its basis. Instruments are for the privileged few. Only the human voice—accessible to all, free of charge and yet the most beautiful of instruments—can be the fertile soil of a musical culture extending to all." Twenty-five years later, in one of his last pedagogical texts, an introduction to the volume entitled *Musical Education in Hungary* (1966, 1969) he stated that: "Our age of mechanization leads along a road ending with man himself as a machine; only the spirit of singing can save us from this fate." The "gold reserve" of his teaching methods lay in the decades of educational activity and the several hundred singing exercises, published in 21 booklets, which the world—and not Kodály himself—together with the numerous articles and essays belonging to it, called the "Kodály Method". Some of the elements of his "method", the development of hearing and rhythm, musical reading and writing, and solmization, were however already known. He himself names his precursors: Curwen, Bertalotti, Guido di Arezzo..., though he was unable to quote Hungarian examples because before him there was only a preponderance of foreign-inspired "school songs" in the teaching curriculum. He had to fight against these, and in the inter-war years, he was in opposition to the official educational authorities. Opposition in itself is of course no teaching method, but he had concepts of his own, which, after the liberation of Hungary in 1945—and now with government support—could at last be put into practice. Under his guidance a system of musical education evolved, which the International Society of Musical Education (ISME), who elected him Honorary President, recommended for introduction to all its member-states.

In the field of musical education Kodály was not a pioneer in the strict sense of the word either. Nevertheless, he was the first to build one coherent, comprehensive and modern method from the many differing traditions, and in doing so, with the full unity of theory and practice he made his system unique. Its theory did not develop from prosaic texts but from the hundreds of little pieces in his musical booklets. "It is the development of instinctive perception and training, and not sophisticated lectures, that bring people nearer to music," he declared in 1937 in the epilogue of *Bicinia Hungarica* I. The compositions for children's choruses created simultaneously with his educational works, are an ultimate conclusion and a shining practical proof of his method.

We have now before us a triple portrait—Kodály the composer, Kodály the musicologist, and Kodály the educationalist. His career can be followed in pictures, but a creative artist—to quote his own words—can be known only from his works, "for in them he deposits the better half of himself".
Kodály (together with Bartók) was the creator of a new Hungarian musical art. In addition he laid the foundations of a general and high-level Hungarian musical culture, as a scholar, an educator, and a loyal son of his people. His activities make out of man an educated being, and out of the masses cultured audiences. In Hungary, therefore, a subjective surplus may be added to the objective values of his lifework. This surplus is one of the reasons why the appreciation of Kodály's music differs to a certain degree in Hungary from abroad. Another reason is inherent in his musical material, which is just as alien to dodecaphony as to the European system of major and minor keys. Its tonal basis separates it from the first, and its pentatonic character separates it from the second. Kodály set out along the road which promised more work and fewer results with no illusions, giving up the other

possibility, which (as proved by his *Adagio* in 1905) promised quicker and greater international success. He did not seek personal originality but endeavoured to express national originality. He found it in the ancient store of Hungarian folksongs. With the discovery and adaptation of folksongs Kodály created something quite different from the neoclassicists' involvement with the past, which was in fact an escape from the burning issues of the present, since he tried to draw strength from the pure source of tradition. The forgotten past gave him strength for the future. His art was humanistic both in aim and content, for Kodály believed in development. He believed that Man and society could be reformed, and stood at all times for progress.

What he accomplished during the early years of the century was revolutionary, both from an artistic and a political point of view. Kodály always remained loyal to the ideals he had proclaimed, and it was for this reason that he refused to participate in the revolutions that were to come in European music: he simply denied that they were necessary. In rejecting attempts which he regarded as self-limiting, or ideas that seemed to be pseudo-progressive, he merely stood up in defense of the still unstabilized values created by him and Bartók.

Today we are able to look at the folklorism-dodecaphony debate from a certain historical perspective and can see not only what separates the two trends but also what connects them: e.g. the intensified use of small musical form, for both trends work with a 'shortwinded' material—the 'folksong', and the 'tone-row' respectively; or the use of the variation principle. Variation is an inherent characteristic not only of folksongs, but also of the twelve-note technique. An instinctive perception of deeper connections (and their conscious disclosure) might lead to a sort of synthesis between the two trends. It would be all the more desirable, so that the gap between modern music and the listening public does not grow even wider.

Thanks to the work of Bartók and Kodály the ancient folksong still survives in the present generation of young Hungarian composers, and since the results of other modern European trends have also taken strong root, we cannot preclude the possibility that a synthesis of the two will eventually materialize in their own country. The basis for this assumption is our conviction that Kodály's teaching and *ars poetica* are still alive. His ability to achieve a synthesis of the apparent contradictions of the two trends may well encourage the younger generation of composers to follow suit. The educating spirit of Kodály, the learned musicologist and man of vision, is also still alive. Many of his publications are still of basic importance in national and international folklore research, and his concept for musical reading and writing and for the musical education of young people and audiences.

But above all, his art is still alive, and still has universal significance, because he undertook to express the truth of his people and his era.

This is what makes Kodály, the national composer, a truly international figure.

1 / Kecskemét. Town Hall Square, about 1880. On the left is the Great Church

"I was born in Kecskemét, but since my parents moved from there when I was but a few months old, the proud name 'Son of Kecskemét' is not really due to me. And yet I was obliged to use it during my wanderings from village to village, for when I was asked where I was from and I said Kecskemét, people's eyes sparkled and they found me sympathetic." (From Kodály's *Reminiscences*, 1966. See Photo Nos. 272–273.)

2 / The station building at the turn of the century. Zoltán Kodály was born here on December 16, 1882, in a wing of the building that has since been pulled down

22

3–4 / His parents. Paulina Jaloveczky (1857–1935) and Frigyes Kodály (1853–1926)

Kodály's father worked for the Hungarian State Railways for forty years (1870–1910). From 1883 he was station-master at Szob, Galánta (Galanta, Czechoslovakia) and Nagyszombat (Trnava, Czechoslovakia). Kodály's mother was one of six children of an impoverished inn-keeper.

They were married in Kecskemét in 1879. They both were fond of music: Kodály's father played the violin while his mother sang and played the piano.

23

"The author spent the happiest seven years of his childhood at Galánta. The Gypsy Band of Galánta, under its leader Mihók, was famous at the time." (Kodály: *Dances from Galánta*. Preface, 1934.) Though the photographs were taken in 1958, the buildings are the same. It was in this village, whose population [2,400] spoke Hungarian, Slovak and German, that the Kodály family lived from 1885 to 1892 (photo Gyula Kertész).

5 / Galánta. The station

6 / "Gypsy Row"

24

7 / THE ELEMENTARY SCHOOL AT GALÁNTA. "MY BAREFOOTED SCHOOLMATES... CHILDREN GIVEN TO BRAWLING OR ROBBING OF BIRD'S NESTS, BUT OTHERWISE COURAGEOUS AND THOROUGH, HONEST BOYS, AND WELL-BEHAVED YOUNG GIRLS AND FOND OF SINGING AND DANCING—WHERE ARE YOU NOW?" THE COMPOSER ASKED SOME FIFTY YEARS LATER (KODÁLY: "BICINIA HUNGARICA". DEDICATION, 1937.)

"The making of my destiny was as natural as breathing. I sang earlier than I talked, and I sang more than I talked. I became acquainted with musical instruments and the classical masterpieces at an early age... I composed first at the age of four..." (Kodály: "Statement", about 1950.)

8 / BECAUSE THE FAMILY WERE OBLIGED TO MOVE FROM PLACE TO PLACE, THE CHILDREN WERE ALL BORN IN DIFFERENT PARTS OF THE COUNTRY: EMILIA, THE ELDEST (1880–1919) IN BUDAPEST; PÁL, THE YOUNGEST (1886–1948) IN GALÁNTA; AND ZOLTÁN IN KECSKEMÉT ON DECEMBER 16, 1882 (PHOTO SÁNDOR FINK)

Nagyszombat, with its historical past, was situated on the western frontier of Hungary and was the scene of Kodály's first serious attempts at studying music. At that time (between 1892 and 1900) Nagyszombat had 12,000 inhabitants, mostly Slovak-speaking, with a minority speaking Hungarian and German.

Kodály learnt to play the piano, violin, viola and cello with very little tuition. Unaided, he attained a standard that enabled him to take part in chamber music at home and in the work of the orchestra at his high school. He also sang in the church choir with his schoolmates.

9 / NAGYSZOMBAT. THE BELFRY, BUILT IN 1574

10 / NAGYSZOMBAT. DRAWINGS OF THE CHURCH OF THE INVALIDS NAMED AFTER ST. JOHN THE BAPTIST, AND THE ARCHIEPISCOPAL HIGH SCHOOL SITUATED IN THE OLD UNIVERSITY BUILDING

He was always among the best pupils at the high school, excelling mainly in literature and languages. However, his interest soon turned to music. He began to compose. His paragons were Haydn and Mozart. "Playing instruments was never the thing for me. I composed more than I played music right from the start," he reminisced later.

11 / NAGYSZOMBAT. THE OLD STREET LEADING TO THE CATHEDRAL

12 / KODÁLY, AS A STUDENT AT NAGYSZOMBAT: WITH HIS BROTHER AND SISTER (PHOTO GYULA BALÁZSOVICH)

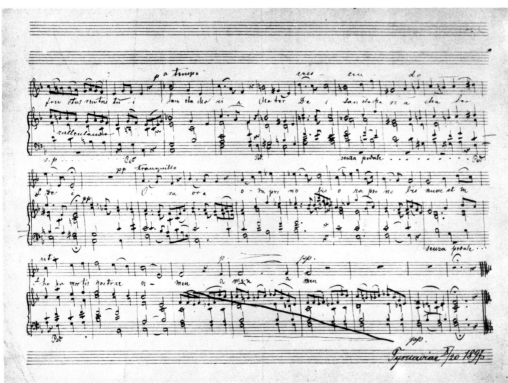

13–14 / One of his first compositions, "Ave Maria", for solo singing voice and organ.
Date: October 20, 1897. (Manuscript)

The high-school orchestra, led by a young teacher, presented Kodály's *Overture* in D Minor in February 1898. They borrowed wind players from the local fire brigade. Since they had no oboist, the oboe part was played by a violin. The composer himself alternately played the cello and beat the drum. The Pozsony newspaper critic was satisfied: "The composition sounded good, and the ideas in it are linked in a logical sequence. The piece indicates a vigorous and dynamic talent." A year later the *Trio* in E-Flat Major—for two violins and a viola—was also performed. The composer played the viola part.

Abonnementspreise des Blattes
für loco mit täglicher Zustellung:

monatlich . . . . . fl. 1.08 = K. 2.16
vierteljährig . . . . „ 3.04 = „ 6.08
halbjährig . . . . „ 6.08 = „ 12.16
ganzjährig . . . . „ 12.16 = „ 24.32

Ohne Zustellung:

monatlich . . . . . fl. —.95 = K. 1.90
vierteljährig . . . . „ 2.85 = „ 5.70
halbjährig . . . . „ 5.70 = „ 11.40
ganzjährig . . . . „ 11.40 = „ 22.80

＊

Mit der dazu gehörigen
„Illustrirten Sonntags-Beilage"
monatlich . . . . . 10 kr. = 20 H. mehr
vierteljährig . . . . 20 „ = 40 „

Westungarischer Grenzbote

Motto: Freiheit und Fortschritt!

Abonnementspreise des Blattes
mit täglicher Postzusendung.
Für das Inland:

monatlich . . . . . fl. 1.20 = K. 2.40
vierteljährig . . . . „ 3.60 = „ 7.20
halbjährig . . . . „ 7.20 = „ 14.46
ganzjährig . . . . „ 14.40 = „ 28.80
Deutschland: viertelj. „ 4.60 = „ 9.20
Schweiz, Italien und
Frankreich: viertelj. . „ 5.60 = „ 11.20

＊

Inserate für Oesterreich-Ungarn
übernehmen die Annoncen-Expeditionen:
Haasenstein & Vogler, Rudolf Mosse und
A. Oppelik in Wien und Budapest.

Inserate für das Ausland
(Frankreich, Deutschland, Belgien, Holland, England
und die Schweiz) übernehmen die Annoncen-Expeditionen von G. L. Daube & Comp. in Frankfurt a. M.
und Haasenstein & Vogler in Hamburg.

Nr. 8738 — Preßburg, Freitag, 25. Feber 1898. — XXVII. Jahrgang.

Das Schülertheater im Tyrnauer Gymnasium.

Mein Weg führte durch Nagy Szombat; wer kennt nicht Nagy-Szombat, das im Jahre 1848 in der vaterländischen Geschichte eine Rolle gespielt, N.-Szombat berühmt durch seine schönen Mädchen und Frauen, berühmt durch seine gegen Lundenburg strebende Bahn, deren Bau, der vor zirka 20 Jahren begonnen, einen so rapiden Fortschritt nahm, daß thatsächlich schon heuer eine Theilstrecke derselben eröffnet wurde.

Ach sehn St., sa... frau, Sonntag gibt... und da könnten Si... wirkt auch mit. Ja... verspricht etwas — ... in N.-Szombat; S... der die meisten grö... setzung gesehen un... dem es als angene... Bedürfniß geworde... Klassiker und der ... vertiefen!

Es kam mir, ... Hausfrau darob ... unwillkürlich eine ... Stuart" in den S... wohnt, und die me... und mir solch' h... daß ich einige Tag...

Und mit Mus... stand vor mir ... Musikbande, die f... artigen Körperschaf... scheidet, daß jeder ... was ihm gefällt, ... volle Gesammtwirk...

erſten künstlerischen Versuche der erwachenden Talente

Die ersten Töne der Ouverture erklangen, das Orchester ist mit Ausnahme der Bläser aus Schülern der Anstalt zusammengestellt, ein junger Professor steht am Dirigentenpult, der die noch ungebändigten Kräfte mit seinem Taktstocke im Zaum halten soll.

Wir lauschen — es klingt hübsch, die Gedanken reih'n sich logisch an einander, es ist Schwung in der Komposizion, sie zeugt von Talent; ich blick in's Program: Ouverture (D moll) komponiert von Zoltán K . . . . Schüler der 4. Klasse. Jetzt verstehe ich die feine Bläse auf den Wangen meiner Nachbarin. Die Ouverture ist zu Ende, ein Beifall braust durch das Theater und Rufe nach dem Kompositeur — die Bläse verschwindet von den Wangen meiner Nachbarin und eine Thräne glitzert im Auge der zärtlichen Mutter, ihr Junge, ihr Sohn von Beifall umrauscht — und ich freue mich herzlich mit ihr. O möge dieses Beifalls-Rauschen meinen Jungen nicht verwirren, möge er bescheiden bleiben und im ernsten Streben ein ganzer Mann werden! Ich verrathe die Gedanken der glücklichen Mutter ja der Beifall ist ein süßes Gift, welches schon manchem jungen Talente zum Verderben geworden ist. Nun folgt „Kemény Simon", geschichtliches Drama in 2 Aufzügen von Karl Kisfaludy, aufgeführt von Schülern der 5. 6. 7. und 8. Klasse. Die jugendlichen Schauspieler haben ihre Rolle gut memorirt und mit Begeisterung dargestellt, ihr sicheres Auftreten ließ den Gedanken gar nicht aufkommen, daß man einer Dilletanten Vorstellung beiwohnt. Als zweites Stück folgte: „Nagybácsi a kosárban" Posse von Robert Wladár, von Zöglingen der 6. 7. und 8. Klasse mit viel Humor aufgeführt, besonders erheiternd wirkten das eingelegte Kouplet von den Röngten Strahlen. Beide Aufführungen lohnte ein Beifallssturm wie solchen nur ein dankbares und begeistertes Publikum spenden kann.

16 / THE 7TH GRADE AT EXAMINATION TIME, JUNE 1899. THE COMPOSER IS THIRD FROM THE LEFT IN THE FRONT ROW

Kodály at the end of his school career: he graduated in June 1900 and left Nagyszombat, for he had to choose a career.

"In our class seven of us graduated with honours," he said half a century later. "In fact all of us could have been high school teachers... I myself knew ancient Greek so well that I could easily have taught it." With his test-paper entitled "A Parallel between Virgil's Aeneis and Homer's Epics" he won the school literary competition. His teachers predicated a "great scholarly future" for him. A lawyer friend of the family suggested the boy should study for the bar, since "a lawyer can become anything". The accepted opinion at the time was that a music-master's career was not a "gentlemanly profession". And so Kodály arrived in Budapest—which then had a population of 700,000—to continue his studies.

17 / FAREWELL TO NAGYSZOMBAT

19 / The new bridge had already been constructed. By paying a toll one could walk across to the Buda side (at Sáros Baths—today Gellért Baths) with its forest-clad hills. On the Pest side of the Danube life was very noisy. Tramways had only recently been put into operation, and Pest also had the first "tube-railroad" on the Continent

Budapest, Ferencz-József hid. — Franz Josefbrücke. 1901 I/39

Although Kodály had no doubts as to his vocation as a composer, for the sake of his parents and to gain a wider intellectual horizon he enrolled at the University to learn Hungarian and German at the Faculty of Philosophy. This faculty and the Eötvös College, organized in a similar way to the French École Normale Supérieure, provided him with a broad education. Kodály continued his studies at the Academy of Music until 1905 and frequently visited the Opera House. "In Pest the official language of music was German and the majority of professional musicians knew no Hungarian... No wonder that in this German world we developed a desire to get to know the real Hungary which could be found nowhere in Pest." (Kodály: "Confession", 1932.)

21 / The old Academy of Music on the Boulevard. Franz Liszt had taught here some 15 years earlier

22 / The Budapest Opera House, centre of the contemporary Hungarian Wagner cult

23 / Ödön Mihalovich (1842–1929), composer, and Director of the Academy of Music from 1887 to 1919 (photo Miklós Labori)

24 / Hans Koessler (1853–1926), Kodály's professor of composition (photo Strelisky)

25 / Viktor Herzfeld (1856–1919), Kodály's professor of history of music and musical theory (photo Terényi)

"Koessler was of the opinion that the Hungarian character should be used only with moderation in serious music, just here and there to provide a dash of colour like in the last movement of Brahms' Piano Quartet." (Kodály: *The Folklorist Bartók*, 1950.) An excellent teacher of Bavarian extraction who never learnt Hungarian, he nevertheless educated a whole series of first-class representatives of Hungarian music.

Three of Koessler's pupils

26 / Béla Bartók

27 / Zoltán Kodály (photo May and Co.)

28 / Ernest Dohnányi (photo Underwood)

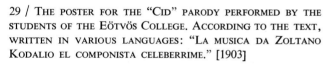

29 / The poster for the "Cid" parody performed by the students of the Eötvös College. According to the text, written in various languages: "La musica da Zoltano Kodalio el componista celeberrime." [1903]

30 / The poster for the "tragedy" performed by the students of the Eötvös College: "A nagybácsi (The Uncle), collected from old memories by Gyuszi Bodnár. Music whistled by Mr. Kodály." [1904]

Kodály's career as "house composer" at the College began in February 1902 when he composed the music for the parody entitled "The Hunchback of Notre Dame". He also conducted the incidental music for all three student plays. According to his recollections [in 1956], the students in the picture are, beginning with the back row standing (from left to right): Ferenc Szolár, László Stockinger, György Tulbure, Kodály, Maróthy, Károly Ringbauer, Gábor Németh. The front row standing: Vass, Gulovics, László Birta (Bartha), Vilmos Scharbert, Endre Kalocsay, István Jakucs, Vilmos Krausz, Miklós Draganau, Gyula Szekfü, Csépke, Gyula Bodnár. Seated: Balogh, Szőke, Bartal, Béla Demeter, Elemér Boreczky, Tibor Gerevich, Gréb, Iván Hajnóczy. On the floor: Endre Gombocz, Kálmán Czógler, Géza Zemplén, Miklós Szabó.

31 / "Conductor Kodály" with the participants at a variety evening during a carnival

32 / During an excursion to Mezőtúr [October 8, 1903]

The amateur orchestra of the high school of this provincial town invited Kodály (third from the right, standing) to play the 'cello and piano at a concert they were giving to commemorate their three hundred and fiftieth anniversary.

33 / During an excursion to Bayreuth [August, 1904]

Károly Gianicelli, a professor at the Academy, and the Budapest representative of the Wagner family (sitting in the middle) took a few outstanding graduates of the Academy of Music on a scholarship to the Bayreuth Festival Plays. Kodály is standing behind him, and on the right in the same row is Imre Kálmán, who later became a popular operetta composer. Kodály was thoroughly acquainted with Wagner's works—he could play the Overture to Tristan from memory on the piano —but was never really influenced by them.

34 / Kodály with Sándor Szilágyi and
Antal Molnár [1904]

35 / Béla Balázs, poet, writer and aesthe-
tician (1884–1949) (photo Emil Keglovich)

The Eötvös College not only provided a suitable environment for the development of one's individual abilities, but also infused its students with a kind of team spirit. Sándor Szilágyi, who as a senior had endeavoured to transplant his own ardour for Wagner into his younger contemporary Kodály, did not forget his colleague when he embarked on a teaching career. He recommended Kodály as a private tutor for one of his high-school pupils who was trying his hand at composing, the then 14-year-old Antal Molnár.

Béla Balázs, Kodály's fellow student and an admirer of the revolutionary poet Endre Ady (1877–1919), was a promising literary talent. His first poems linked him with the symbolists, and his first drama was one of philosophical inspiration. He wrote the libretti for two of Bartók's stage works: *Bluebeard's Castle* and *The Wooden Prince*. His endeavours towards a synthesis of the ancient Hungarian folk ballad with new trends were not dissimilar to those of Kodály—perhaps they even stemmed partly from him.

36 / The first "free year in Buda" (1904–1905) after the College years gave rise to great plans and decisions. Kodály taught, composed, wrote theses and prepared for his doctorate in philosophy

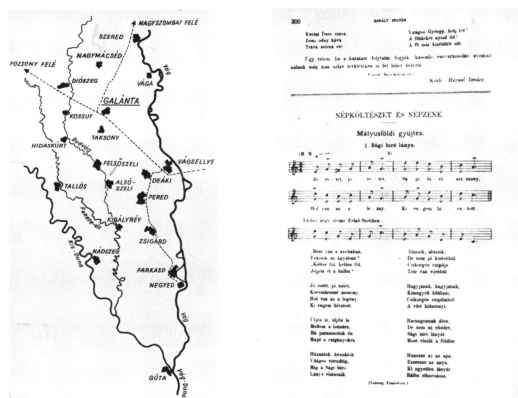

Kodály, having studied the existing collections of folksongs as well as Béla Vikár's phonograph recordings, set out, in August 1905, to collect and notate unadulterated folksongs as he heard them from peasant singers. He began his work in Galánta and continued in the neighbouring villages. In one month he collected a hundred and fifty tunes in this area. He published thirteen of these in the periodical *Ethnographia*, under the title "Mátyusföld Collection". When all the material that was accessible to him had been collected—about a thousand songs—he wrote his dissertation under the title *The Stanzaic Structure of Hungarian Folksong* (1906).

Kodály's creative alliance with Béla Bartók (1881–1945) came about in the wake of this work. Their art and musical activities so inter-related and yet at the same time so dissimilar, complemented each other in the realization of a common musical goal. "Their friendship stemmed from their common musical ideal, and the memory of this... is preserved forever in their work." (Mrs. Bartók, Ditta Pásztory, 1972). What was this common ideal? "...The vision of an educated Hungary, reborn from the people rose before us. We decided to devote our lives to its realization." (Kodály: *The Memory of Bartók*, 1955.)

39 / KODÁLY AND BARTÓK, ONE OF THEIR EARLIEST PICTURES TOGETHER (1908). IN THE BACKGROUND IS MRS. GRUBER, EMMA SÁNDOR, THEIR COMMON PUPIL, WHO BROUGHT THEM TOGETHER

In the Zobor area north-west of Mátyusföld lives a very ancient Hungarian tribe. Kodály recorded their traditional folk tunes—for the first time—using a phonograph. His plan to collect folksongs at the geographical boundary where two languages "meet" was also taken up by Bartók. "In order to work systematically we divided the various fields of research between us," Kodály wrote. "We often met and each brought with him the results of his collecting in a knapsack. We put together and compared what each of us had discovered separately..." They subsequently published twenty folksongs to get the public acquainted with folk music. In the preface to the volume Kodály was critical of Hungarian audiences: "The overwhelming majority are not yet Hungarian enough, and are no longer naive enough and yet at the same time not cultured enough to accept these folksongs. 'Hungarian folksongs in the concert hall!' Today it seems rather strange for such material to be included among the masterpieces of musical literature and—foreign folksongs! But the time will come." By the time the volume appeared Kodály was already in Berlin with Béla Balázs on a study tour (December 1906—April 1907). He then spent three months in Paris. His greatest experience was the discovery of Debussy's music.

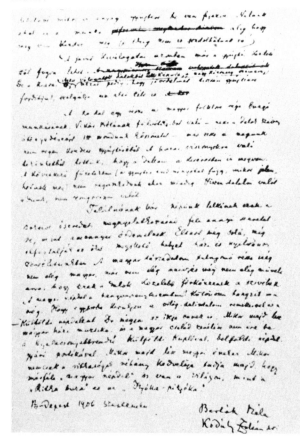

43 / The new building of the Budapest Academy of Music in Liszt Ferenc Square, inaugurated in 1907

44 / The two new teachers at the Academy, Bartók and Kodály

Bartók began to teach piano at the Academy in the early part of 1907, as successor to his former master, István Thomán, who was once a pupil of Franz Liszt. Kodály began his activities as a teacher of musical theory. On the basis of his experiences gained in Paris he was particularly concerned with aural training and dictation. For the former he made use of the exercises of Bertalotti, and for the latter—as a daring innovation—he used folksongs.

41 / The preface to the first joint publication of folksongs. Kodály's draft [September 1906]

42 / Title-page of the first edition of "Hungarian Folksongs" [December, 1906]

They were Kodály's first co-workers. From 1910 onwards, they actively participated in the tremendous programme of Hungarian folk-music research. Antal Molnár undertook the lion's share of the work of modernizing the teaching of solfege.

47 / A page from the Fantasia movement of the "Sonata for 'Cello and Piano" (op. 4), composed in 1909–10. The composer's manuscript. The "Sonata" was first performed by Jenő Kerpely and Béla Bartók. It was subsequently premiered in 1910–1912 in Paris and Berlin

48 / THE WALDBAUER-KERPELY QUARTET, WHO GOT TOGETHER IN ORDER TO PERFORM THE MUSIC OF
BARTÓK AND KODÁLY (PHOTO BY ALADÁR SZÉKELY)

Most of the older musicians did not want, or were not able, to get acquainted with the new
music, and the more famous ones would not risk their popularity. But these four enthusiastic
and conscientious young musicians (the sum total of the ages of the members of the quartet
was only 81 years) stood by the two composers. They held about one hundred rehearsals for
two special performances that were to take place on 17 and 19 March, 1910. From left to
right: Bartók, János Temesváry (second violin), Antal Molnár (viola), Imre Waldbauer (first
violin), Kodály, and Jenő Kerpely (cello).
During the same year, Kodály's compositions were performed in both Zurich and Paris.
In Paris—according to Bartók who was present—it was "a sensation, for a complete stranger
emerged before the audience as one of the foremost composers".

49 / Emma Sándor (photo Károly Koller's successors)

The marriage they contracted on 3 August 1910, which lasted for forty-nine years, was an example of perfect harmony. Mrs. Kodály was herself a gifted composer, who had won competitions and prizes in London and Paris. Some of her themes were elaborated by Kodály, Bartók and Dohnányi. She was also an excellent translator. She translated the texts of many of Kodály's vocal compositions into German.

50 / Zoltán Kodály

Bartók's wedding gift to the Kodálys was the third piece of his Seven Sketches for piano (op. 9), the Lento, dedicated "To Emma and Zoltán".

51–52 / Two pages from the notebook in which Kodály wrote down folksongs

The County of Nyitra proved to be a treasure-trove of old folksongs. Kodály paid frequent visits to the region: In January 1911 he recorded Slovak folksongs in the village of Szalakusz (Salakúzy, Czechoslovakia), and Hungarian folksongs at Menyhe (Mechenice, Czechoslovakia).

46

53 / The second Transylvanian folksong collecting tour, in 1912. Before the Calvinist Church in Körösfő (Crişeni, Rumania)

54 / Kodály, Mrs. Kodály and Bartók sitting in front of a carved wooden door-frame in nearby Magyargyerőmonostor (Mănăstireni, Rumania)

It was in this region that the famous Kalotaszeg peasant embroidery was done. It was an established centre for folk art and folk music and, because of the preservation of its old traditions, was a treasure-trove for folklorists.

55 / Kodály at the organ of the Körösfő Church

56–57 / COUNTRY WALKS

Kodály was a great lover of nature. He would roam around the countryside both in winter and summer, always wearing the same cape. He was also fond of sport, particularly gymnastics, swimming, tennis and in winter, skating or skiing. He believed that longevity was not just an inherited thing and could best be achieved through determination, and that the basis for it was to lead a healthy and active life.

58 / MAKING THE ACQUAINTANCE OF A TORTOISE 59 / VIAREGGIO, 1912

The two pictures and the drawing are by Mrs. Kodály. She could have become a good photographer as well as a fine graphic artist; she could create character and atmosphere with just a few lines.

60 / ON AN EXCURSION
IN THE HILLS OF BUDA

61 / Kodály on holiday in Switzerland

62 / In the mountains in Hungary

63 / Towards Languard

Kodály preferred to spend his holidays in the mountains. He not only longed for the pure air, but the magical atmosphere of mountains also appealed to him. "The mountains have a voice," he said on more than one occasion. It was this voice he recalled in Mountain Nights, the choruses without words for female voice. Before the First World War he rambled a great deal in Switzerland during the summers.

As the folksong collecting progressed the problem of classifying and publishing the material emerged. Kodály and Bartók drafted a plan for a new universal collection of folksongs in which Kodály expounded the strict editorial principles involved in compiling a Hungarian "Corpus Musicae Popularis". The main body of the material was to be made up of the tunes they themselves had collected (after eight years these had already exceeded three thousand) and to these were to be added the collections of their co-workers and Béla Vikár. The plan of 1913 was never realized. The first volume of the "Corpus Musicae Popularis Hungaricae", *Children's Games*, finally appeared in 1951. Bartók and Kodály also showed each other their new compositions. "I owe it to his astoundingly sure and astute musical judgement that many of my works were finally put into a more perfect form", Bartók said of Kodály in 1921. Kodály was already professor of composition at the Liszt Ferenc Academy of Music—the successor of Koessler, who had retired.

66 / Four-hand music on the piano in Kodály's home, in Áldás utca. The drawing is by Mrs. Kodály

67 / BEFORE HIS DESK AT HOME

68 / READING A GOOD BOOK AT AN OPEN WINDOW

69 / ÁLDÁS UTCA IN WINTER

From 1910 until the end of 1924, the Kodálys lived on the second floor of a house built on the Rózsadomb (Hill of Roses) surrounded by the Buda Hills, and far from the noise of the town. The window offered a magnificent view, and the garden below was lovely. The surroundings encouraged creative work, and the years spent there were rich in songs and chamber-pieces.

One of Kodály's last collecting tours before the war took him to Bukovina, a Rumanian district, lying beyond Hungary's eastern frontier. In April 1914 he noted down more than two hundred folksongs from Hungarians who lived in five of the local villages. The folksongs of Józseffalva's Rumanian population also aroused his interest; he wrote down or recorded numerous "hora" and "colinda" tunes. The real treasure house of folk music was Istensegíts. It was here that the most folksongs in their original form were preserved. Kodály also recorded folk customs and children's games in the photographs he took there.

71 / "Tyúkozás". A singing game played by girls in Istensegíts (Zoltán Kodály's photo)

At the news of the outbreak of war the Kodálys interrupted their tour of Switzerland and started for home. Kodály wrote about their journey—and the origin of the Duo for Violin and Cello (op. 7)—to Jenő Léner (1895–1948), first violinist of the world-famous string quartet which bore his name: "We had to complete the last stage of our journey to the Swiss border in a freight car, as Switzerland was also mobilizing. We were forced to stay in a Tyrolean border village for a few days. It was here that the vision of the Duo suddenly came to me. Never before had I thought about composing for this combination... music manuscript paper was not available in Feldkirch, and this is the reason why the first movement which at that time I wrote practically unchanged is in a school manuscript book. So the Duo grew out of this kind of experience. Whether others will ever perceive in it even a vague notion of the unpending war or the indescribable grandness of the gigantic mountains, remains a big question." (Letter to Léner, c. 1922.)

73 / On the way home the smile of a little girl in Feldkirch, Adelheid, brightens the spirits of the Kodálys [July 1914]

74 / KODÁLY, IN CIVILIAN CLOTHES STANDING BETWEEN TWO SOLDIERS [1916]

His two cousins Béla and Kornél Jaloveczky both served in the Hungarian army during the war, whereas Kodály, as a high-school teacher, was exempted.
The militia was set up to guard strategical points and public buildings in Budapest. During the first year of the war, Kodály was assigned to the group guarding the Buda Tunnel.

75 / IN THE VOLUNTEERS' MILITIA. [THIRD FROM LEFT IN THE FIRST ROW, 1915]

Folksong collecting did not cease during the war either. Kodály, along with Bartók, sought permission to continue their musical research within the army. They obtained official permission in March, 1916. Kodály collected soldiers' songs in the summer in Kassa, Zemplén and Szabolcs, and in the autumn and winter he travelled to Nagyszalonta to find the original folk melodies to complement the folk text collection sent previously to the Kisfaludy Society.

77 / Nativity players of Nagyszalonta (Zoltán Kodály's photo)

78 / "I was not born to be a practising instrumental virtuoso..." [Kodály]

79 / Kodály with a born instrumentalist, virtuoso Ernest Dohnányi, in the garden

80 / Béla Bartók with his mother and Mrs. Kodály in Áldás utca [1917–18]

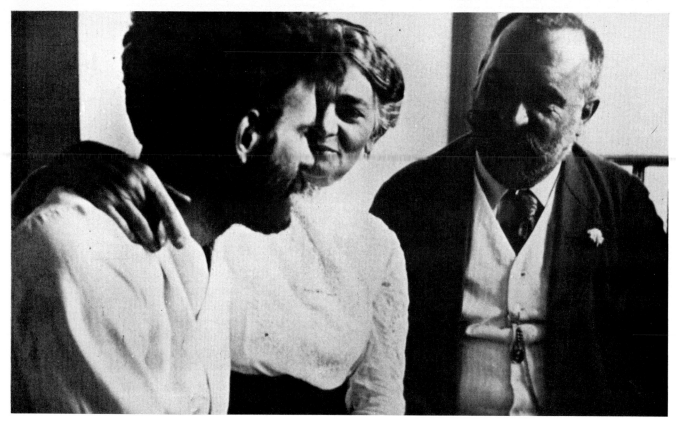

81 / A FAMILY VISIT TO ÁLDÁS UTCA. KODÁLY WITH HIS MOTHER AND UNCLE, VIKTOR JALOVECZKY

Kodály's father retired at the end of 1910 (after forty years of service) and moved to Budapest with his wife in the summer of 1913. An ever more frequent visitor of the Kodálys towards the end of the war was Béla Reinitz (1878–1943), who had just been demobilized from the army at that time. Reinitz was a critic with an appreciation of new Hungarian music, and was the first composer to set poems of Endre Ady to music. He discussed with the Kodálys the reforms that were necessary in Hun-garian musical life.

82 / BÉLA REINITZ VISITING THE KODÁLYS (1917–1918)

83 / KODÁLY WITH BARTÓK AND IOAN BUŞIŢIA AT BIHARFÜRED IN THE SUMMER OF 1918
(PHOTO BY MRS. ZOLTÁN KODÁLY)

In the last year of the war the Kodálys and Bartók went to Biharfüred (Stîna de Vale, Rumania) for a short holiday. Their excursion to the picturesque "Miracle Spring" was arranged by Ioan Buşiţia (1875–1953), teacher at the Belényes (Beiuş) secondary school, and friend of Bartók.

84 / PAGE 1 OF SONG 3 OF THE "LATE MELODIES" (OP. 6). THE COMPOSER'S MANUSCRIPT

85 / THE SONG-WRIT
(PHOTO BY IRÉN WE

The title *Late Melodies* suggests that Kodály drew inspiration from old Hungarian poetry. In fact, of the seven poems set to music, four were by Dániel Berzsenyi (1776–1836), two by Ferenc Kölcsey (1790–1838), and one by Mihály Csokonai Vitéz (1773–1805). In another group of compositions (*Five Songs,* op. 9), he drew inspiration from the contemporary poets Endre Ady (1877–1919) and Béla Balázs. The songs are not only a fine example of Kodály's epical and lyrical abilities but at the same time his musical portrayals show a deep feeling for the work of the two poets.

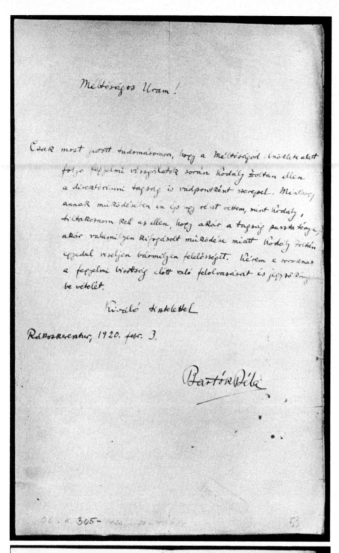

During the revolutionary period after the lost war, beginning November 1918, the course of Hungarian musical life was largely determined by Béla Reinitz. He organized a musical "Directory" of three members—Bartók, Dohnányi and Kodály. In February 1919 he appointed Dohnányi Director of the Academy, and appointed Kodály Deputy Director. After the fall of the Hungarian Republic of Councils, Reinitz was forced to go into exile, while Kodály was suspended from office and subjected to disciplinary proceedings. This was when Bartók wrote to the chairman of the Disciplinary Committee about his Directory activities: "...I protest against Zoltán Kodály alone undertaking any responsibility either for the mere fact of being a member, or for any other activity [in the Directory]."

86–87 / Two letters of protest written by Bartók and Dohnányi

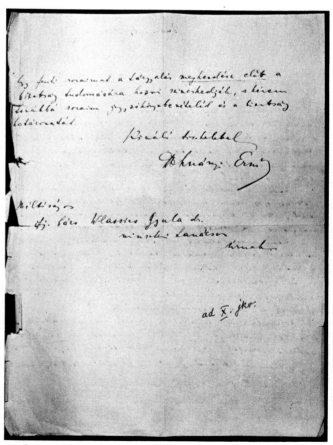

Dohnányi also replied to the charges levelled against him in connection with the administration of the Academy: "I declare myself in full solidarity with Kodály, and undertake full responsibility for the measures taken under my directorship."

Kodály's bold attitude also commands respect. "Let him dare face me and censure me," he declared, "who worked more than I for Hungary. All the work I undertook was unsupported by the State, in fact I funded it from my own resources." Although he was acquitted of the accusation, his appointment as Deputy Director was annulled, and the persecution against him continued. For two years he was not permitted to teach at the Academy. During those difficult times two prominent representatives of the younger generation stood by him, supporting his principles and his art in their essays and articles.

88 / ALADÁR TÓTH (1898–1968), MUSIC CRITIC

89 / BENCE SZABOLCSI (1899–1973), MUSICOLOGIST

90/ THE MASTER AND HIS PUPILS. ON A FAREWELL EXCURSION IN THE BUDA HILLS WITH HIS STUDENTS IN JUNE, 1925. FROM LEFT TO RIGHT, ISTVÁN SZELÉNYI, MIHÁLY SZIGETI, GYULA KERTÉSZ, LAJOS BÁRDOS, KODÁLY, GYÖRGY KERÉNYI, MÁTYÁS SEIBER, JENŐ ÁDÁM AND ANTAL DORÁTI

During his enforced absence his students took private lessons from him at his home. He resumed his teaching duties at the Academy in 1921, and the subsequent attack in the press following his students' diploma concert made Kodály defend his pupils and justify his principles of teaching: "...we must assimilate all the values of the Western European musical heritage... However, we must produce not only European, but also at the same time Hungarian musicians... Only the amalgamation of both European and Hungarian heritage can bring about a result which will have meaning for Hungarians as well... We no longer wish to be subjected to musical colonialism. We do not want to ape an alien musical culture."

91 / THE MASTER AND HIS PUPILS, AS THE CARTOONIST JÓZSEF HANÁK SAW THEM. FROM LEFT TO RIGHT: BENCE SZABOLCSI, TIBOR SERLY, KODÁLY, GÉZA FRID AND PÁL HERMANN. IN THE FIGURE MINUS THE HEAD, THE CARTOONIST DREW A CARICATURE OF HIMSELF

92 / THE FIRST YEARS OF PEACE. KODÁLY IN SALZBURG IN THE COMPANY OF VIOLIN VIRTUOSO ZOLTÁN SZÉKELY, EMIL HERTZKA, DIRECTOR OF THE VIENNESE UNIVERSAL EDITION AND OTHER REPRESENTATIVES OF INTERNATIONAL MUSICAL LIFE

"After World War I the two sides still looked daggers at each other, but the musicians were already gathering in Salzburg to shake hands with their former enemies... It turned out of course that they never were enemies... Musicians have an unshakable faith in universal brotherhood..." (Kodály: *On Peace,* 1951.) At the first chamber-music festival of the International Society of New Music, founded in Salzburg in 1922, the presentation of Kodály's *Sonata* (op. 8) and his *Trio Serenade* (op. 12) was considered a great event.

93 / SALZBURG FESTIVAL, AUGUST, 1923. KODÁLY IN THE COMPANY OF JOACHIM STUTCHEWSKY, RUSSIAN BORN SWISS CELLIST, AND THE POLISH BORN AMERICAN COMPOSER LOUIS GRUENBERG

King David's lamentations, the grief of Mihály Kecskeméti Vég, the 16th-century Hungarian preacher and poet,
and Kodály's own bitterness, are combined to create a
work of staggering force. It was composed at the same
time as Bartók's *Dance Suite* and Dohnányi's *Festive
Overture*, at the request of the Municipality. The aldermen wanted to celebrate the 50th anniversary of the
foundation of Budapest—the amalgamation of Pest, Buda
and Óbuda—with the performance of these compositions
(on 19 November, 1923). The words chosen by Kodály
may have sounded strange to the ears of the aldermen:
"This whole city is laden with anger... There is not
another like it, it is so full of perfidy..."

95–96 / THE FIRST AND LAST PAGES OF THE "PSALMUS", IN THE COMPOSER'S OWN HANDWRITING

97 / A PORTRAIT OF KODÁLY BY VIOLIN VIRTUOSO EMIL TELMÁNYI'S FIRST WIFE, THE ARTIST ANNE MARIE CARL-NIELSEN [1925]

98 / A PHOTOGRAPH OF KODÁLY BY VIOLINIST STEFI GEYER [ZURICH, 1926]

99 / A PHOTOGRAPH TAKEN BY VIOLIN VIRTUOSO ZOLTÁN SZÉKELY [NIJMEGEN, 1927]

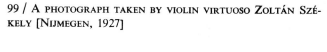

Kodály's international career—interrupted by the First World War—began again with the performances of the *Psalmus Hungaricus* conducted by Andreas Volkmar in Zurich on June 17 and 18, 1926. This same composition started his career as a conductor too. He first conducted the *Psalmus* in April, 1927 at the Concertgebouw, Amsterdam. After these successes the invitations began to arrive.

100–101 / The first stage scenes of "Háry János" (designed by Gusztáv Oláh)

102 / The poster announcing the first
performance of "Háry János"

In *Háry* elements of true historical character and of popular imagination are
combined: it is a legend that is truer
than history.

"I do not know how far I succeeded,"
Kodály said in an interview given on
the day of the dress rehearsal, "but I
do know that the songs are good, and
from the first to the last, in true folk
tradition... They are more apt on the
lips of the singers, than the use of any
individual sentiment. They are pearls,
only the setting is of my making.
I strove hard to be worthy of them.
To the best of my knowledge this is
the first time that the songs of the Hungarian people have been heard on the
stage of the Opera House..."

103 / KODÁLY IN LEIPZIG. [NOVEMBER, 1927]
(PHOTO BY HOENISCH)

Following its success in Switzerland and Holland, *Psalmus Hungaricus* was also performed in Germany, Austria and England. Kodály presented the *Psalmus* in Leipzig conducting the Gewandhaus Orchestra, in Cambridge conducting the London Symphony and in London conducting the BBC Symphony Orchestra. In Vienna Anton Webern performed the work, and in New York Willem Mengelberg. 1927 marked the beginning of the world-wide understanding of Kodály's music. The following year at the invitation of Sir Ivor Atkins (1869–1953) the composer was a guest at Gloucester; the *Psalmus* was performed at the "Three Choirs Festival".

104 / WITH ATKINS ,A CONDUCTOR FROM WORCESTER [1928]

On October 10 and 12, 1928, Arturo Toscanini (1867–1957) conducted the *Psalmus* in moving and dramatic performances at the Scala in Milan. He himself perfected the Italian translation of the work. Kodály and Toscanini spent the day between the two concerts together at Como. A life-long friendship began between the two musicians.

106 / Toscanini with the Kodálys [Como, 1928]

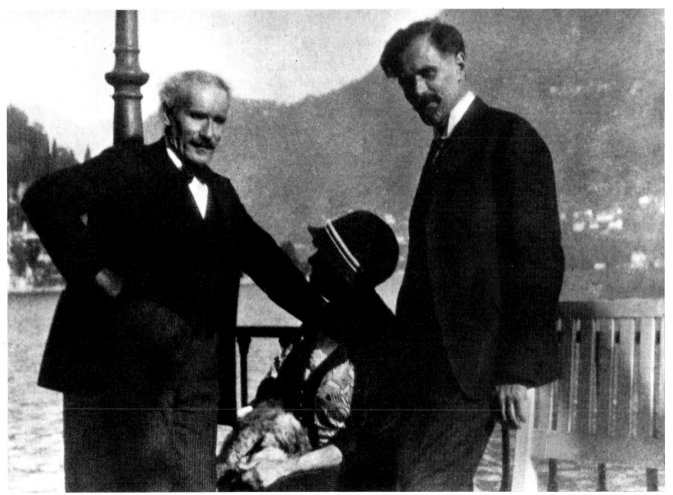

107 / The composer at the time of his first great international successes

"I first composed this work in 1906. After two performances it went by the board. If I have now succeeded in repairing what I messed up when I was half my present age, I owe it to the help of a great *maestro*. He awakened in me the sense of responsibility, the eternal dissatisfaction which prompts one to start everything over again." (From the preface to the score dedicated to Toscanini.)

"He, to whom it is not immaterial what will happen in this country in the way of music in a generation or two," wrote Kodály, "cannot pass a school from which singing is heard with indifference... What they sing, falls as a rule outside the field of art, and the way they sing, is far from being natural... But the Hungarian audience and public should at last be roused from its musical indifference. This can only be started in school."

110 / THE DRAFT OF THE ARTICLE ENTITLED "CHILDREN'S CHORUSES" [1929]

112 / KECSKEMÉT, HIS BIRTHPLACE, WAS AMONG THE FIRST TO JOIN THE GROWING "SINGING YOUTH" MOVEMENT [MARCH 1930]. ON THE LEFT OF KODÁLY ARE ALADÁR TÓTH AND THE CHORAL CONDUCTOR ZOLTÁN VÁSÁRHELYI

He wrote the first concise summary of his twenty-five years of folklore research for the *Musical Encyclopaedia*, edited by Bence Szabolcsi and Aladár Tóth. On the basis of the melodies collected—about 15,000 if one includes all the variations—he declared: "Two major groups, each with its specific and easily distinguishable style, stand out. The first is the type based on the pentatonic scale. This should be regarded as the most ancient stratum of the entire Hungarian stock of melodies. The second is the melody style of the youth. It may have originated—as can be deduced from the ancient tunes—from the amalgamation of different styles, that took place in the eighteenth and nineteenth centuries... Several elements of the pentatonic scale can be found in it, and even its heptatonic scales have a specific Hungarian phraseology... These two kinds contrast mostly with the music of the neighbouring peoples."

113 / THE DRAFT OF AN ARTICLE ENTITLED "HUNGARIAN FOLK MUSIC" [1931]

114 / FOR THE SECOND EDITION OF THE ENCYCLOPAEDIA A NEW MUSICAL EXAMPLE IS INCLUDED AT THE BEGINNING OF THE ARTICLE—THE HUNGARIAN "PEACOCK MELODY" AND ITS CHEREMIS VARIANT (1941)

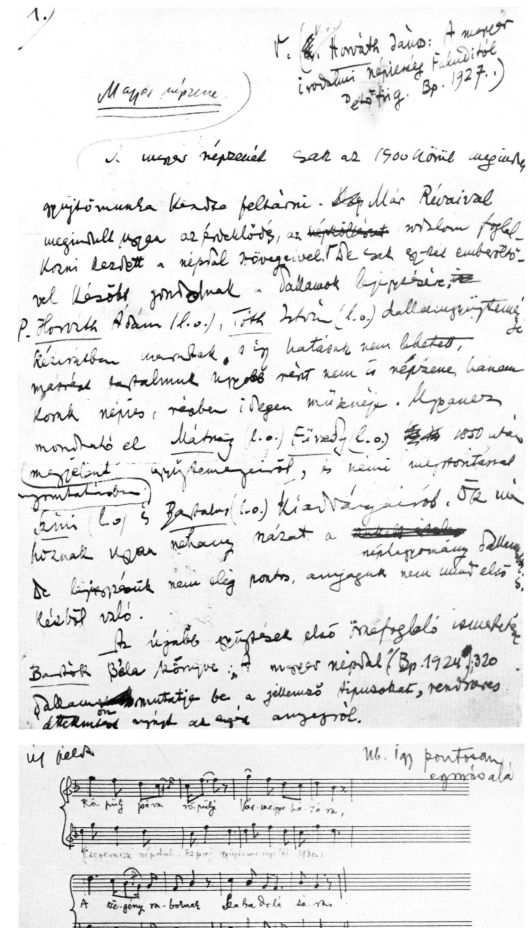

115 / THE COMPOSER OF "THE SPINNING ROOM" [1932] (PHOTO BY ALADÁR SZÉKELY)

116 / THE FIRST PAGE OF THE PIANO SCORE OF "THE SPINNING ROOM". THE COMPOSER'S MANUSCRIPT

117 / A DRAMATIC SCENE FROM THE OPERA (PERFORMED ON APRIL 24, 1932), "THE BALLAD OF ILONA GÖRÖG"

118 / Conductor Sergio Failoni, Kodály and Imre Palló, who, after the title role of Háry János, sang the part of the suitor in "The Spinning Room" (photo by Károly Escher)

"Hungarian scene from Transylvania"— the composer's definition of the genre. He wanted to be a loyal representative of his people: he selected not only the tunes but the full text too, from Hungarian folk poetry.

119 / A few months after the first performance in Budapest, the Scala of Milan also performed "The Spinning Room". Here too, Failoni was responsible for its success

120 / THE FIFTY-YEAR-OLD COMPOSER IN HIS NEW HOME: FROM THE END OF 1924 UNTIL HIS DEATH, HE LIVED AT 89, ANDRÁSSY ÚT (TODAY KODÁLY KÖRÖND)

It was at this time that Kodály completed the series entitled *Hungarian Folksongs*, which comprised ten booklets in which he arranged 57 ballads and folksongs for voice and piano. After the *Dances of Marosszék* he began work on the *Dances from Galánta*. On December 16, 1932 the Hungarian musical establishment celebrated his birthday for the first time with a gala concert of his works.

121 / FROM AMONG HIS PUPILS AND FOLLOWERS, THE PARTICIPANTS OF THE GALA CONCERT. FROM LEFT TO RIGHT—OSZKÁR KÁLMÁN, ONE OF THE FIRST PERFORMERS OF HIS SONGS; ZOLTÁN HORUSITZKY, COMPOSER AND PIANIST; GYÖRGY KERÉNYI, COMPOSER AND FOLK-MUSIC RESEARCHER; JENŐ ÁDÁM, COMPOSER, CONDUCTOR AND TEACHER; FERENC SZÉKELYHIDY, THE FIRST KING DAVID OF THE "PSALMUS"; VIKTOR KARVALY, CONDUCTOR AND IMRE PALLÓ, THE FIRST HÁRY

A long with his fast-growing international reputation, Kodály found he was more and more busy. Despite this, he still found time, even in the 1930s, to maintain contact with nature and simple country people. One of his trips took him to the Tátra Mountains, another to a company of singers and dancers called the Gyöngyös Bokréta *(Pearly Bouquet)*. In 1931 companies such as this had been founded all over the country by Béla Paulini, the writer of the libretto for Háry, to keep alive folk customs that were dying out.

123 / KODÁLY WITH PAULINI AMONG FOLK SINGERS AND DANCERS

This ancient melody occupies a central place in Kodály's compositions. In 1937 he composed a chorus for the Jubilee of the Association of Hungarian Workers' Choirs, based on a revolutionary poem by Endre Ady, which is a paraphrase of this folksong. At the March Front demonstration concert in November 1937 which rallied the left-wing forces, this work became the symbol of protest against the right-wing, pro-German policy of Hungary. And when a year later the reactionary Hungarian police banned the inflammatory chorus, he composed a series of variations based on it for the Concertgebouw Orchestra of Amsterdam. Later on he also arranged it for mixed-voice chorus, so that the song could proclaim:

> Shadowing the prison,
> Peacocks upward flying,
> Brought to silent captives
> Hope, when hope was dying.

126 / At Nagykőrös he conducts the four-part canon, "Song of Faith", in a performance by a thousand-member choir. The Berzsenyi poem set to music in 1936 soon became the revolutionary slogan of the "Singing Youth". [May 1938]

Another of his works which dated from 1936 is the *Te Deum,* which he composed for the 250th anniversary of the recapture of Buda from the Turks and which he himself conducted on several occasions. This grandiose composition for solo quartet, mixed chorus, orchestra and organ, was "sister" to the *Psalmus.*

127 / The composer and conductor in Gloucester Cathedral; the "Te Deum" was an overwhelming success at the "Three Choirs Festival" [September 1937]

128 / KODÁLY IN THE COMPANY OF SÁNDOR VIKÁR AND ZOL-
TÁN VÁSÁRHELYI, TWO LEADERS OF THE HUNGARIAN YOUTH
CHORUS MOVEMENT, DURING THE INTERMISSION OF A CONCERT
GIVEN IN NAGYKŐRÖS BY THE "SINGING YOUTH" MOVEMENT
ON SEPTEMBER 17, 1939 (PHOTO GYULA CSETE)

While the *Psalmus* and the *Te Deum*, the *Háry Suite*,
Summer Evening, Dances of Marosszék and the *Dances
from Galánta* were being presented by the world's
greatest conductors, and were assured of success wherever
they went, Kodály himself was travelling around Hungary in the service of Hungarian musical culture: he
founded choral festivals and inaugurated competitions for
the collecting of folksongs. At the same time he initiated
a pronunciation competition at the Budapest University
to promote Hungarian speech and diction.

129 / THE FIRST FOLKSONG COLLECTING COMPETITION WAS HELD ON JUNE 7, 1939, AT THE TEACHERS' TRAINING COLLEGE IN RANOLDER
UTCA. KODÁLY AWARDED PRIZES TO THE PUPILS WHO COLLECTED THE LARGEST NUMBER OF BEAUTIFUL FOLKSONGS

130 / The farewell concert of Béla Bartók and Ditta Pásztory at the Academy of Music, Budapest on October 8, 1940. János Ferencsik conducted the Budapest Symphony Orchestra. The programme contained piano concertos by Bach and Mozart as well as a few piano pieces from Bartók's Mikrokosmos

Two days later the Bartóks said good-bye to the Kodálys and two days after that they left the country. On October 30 they arrived in New York. Bartók was unable to endure the stifling atmosphere of advancing Nazism. To emigrate, however, was a decision hard to reach for him. In a letter written to Sándor Veress on the 3rd of June, 1939 he revealed his worries: "If somebody stays here even though he had the chance to leave, he can be said to have tacitly agreed with everything that is taking place here. And this cannot even be refuted publicly, for it would only lead to trouble and staying here would become pointless. On the other hand, it could also be said that however bad the country's situation becomes it is everybody's duty to stay at home and help as much as one can."

In the given situation the decision was a particularly difficult one to make, for neither solution could bring about complete satisfaction. Perhaps for this reason too, it was inevitable that if one of them left, the other one should stay at home. With Bartók's departure the preparation of the collection of folksongs for the press was left to Kodály. He had already moved to the Academy of Sciences. At the Academy of Music he retained only the Chair of the College of Hungarian Folk Music.

131–132 / THE 59-YEAR-OLD COMPOSER IN HIS SUMMER HOME AT VÖLGY UTCA [1941] (PHOTO BY MARIANNE GÁCH)

133 / IN THE GARDEN (PHOTO BY MARIANNE GÁCH)

The news of Hungary's disastrous declaration of war on the Soviet Union reached Kodály in his quiet solitude. His message to the world was contained partly in the *Concerto* composed for the 50th anniversary of the Chicago Symphony Orchestra, and which was given its first performances by Frederick Stock; and partly in the preface to the fourth booklet of the *Bicinia Hungarica*, the 57 Cheremis folksongs: "*A few songs still sound the same today along the Danube and the Volga, across a distance of fifteen hundred years and three thousand kilometres...*" He then issued the following motto: "*The Singing Youth movement has no regard for distinctions of class or sections of the population. Music belongs to everybody.*"

84

134 / At the Nyíregyháza Festival of "Singing Youth", with Sándor Vikár and Lajos Bárdos, in May 1942

The year 1942 was declared "Kodály Year" by the National Association of Hungarian Choral Societies. Schools and workers' choruses honoured him with a national festival and the Ethnographic Society presented him with a memorial volume. Kodály—after 35 years of service—formally retired, but in practice he continued working relentlessly. He composed a number of choruses and arranged *Mónár Anna* and *Kádár Kata*, the two most beautiful Székely folk ballads, for voice and small orchestra. However, he devoted most of his time to young people. He wrote two-part singing exercises, published the *333 Reading Exercises*, edited two volumes of *Songs for Schools* together with György Kerényi, and compiled eight booklets of the songbook *SOL–MI* for elementary schools in collaboration with Jenő Ádám.

135–136 / Two memorial plaquettes by Ö. Fülöp Beck and György Edvi Illés in honour of his 60th birthday

137–138 / Visiting friends in the country: with Imre Palló at Pánd; with Endre Rösler and Hugó Kelen at Tárnok. Endre Rösler took over the solo part in the "Psalmus" from Székelyhidy (photo by Marianne Gách, 1942)

At the Budapest Vigadó (Concert Hall) Kodály's works were to be heard more and more frequently. Ansermet conducted *Summer Evening* on May 3, 1941, and Furtwängler *The Peacock* on February 22, 1943.

140 / WITH WILHELM FURTWÄNGLER (PHOTO BY KÁROLY ESCHER)

141 / In 1942 the Hungarian Choir Publishers released Kodály's "Choruses for Children's and Women's Voices" in a bound volume at the Book Fair of that year. The composer dedicates his work at the Academy of Music. Among his pupils György Antal is on the right (Photo by Marianne Gách)

142 / Reading proof-sheets in the engraving shop of Mr. Jatzkó [1943]

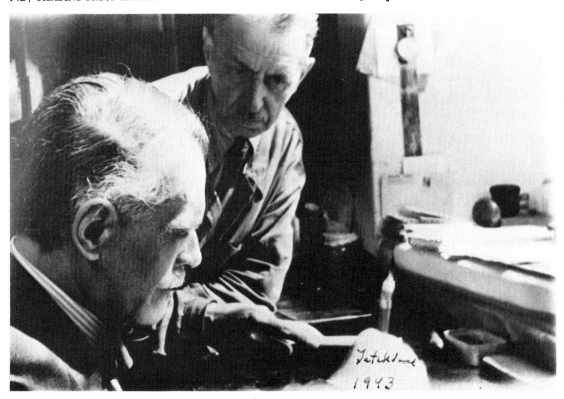

The war was approaching its end. Hitler had occupied Hungary, dragging the country along with him towards certain destruction. Kodály turned for solace to Petőfi, the great poet of the Hungarian struggle for independence in 1848: he protested against the reign of terror by setting to music the following poems: *Battle Song, To the Székelys, Still, By a Miracle, Our Country Stands* and *The Son of an Enslaved Country*. With his choruses entitled *Gentle Entreaty* and *Hymn of Advent* he gave hope to those who were despairing. Meanwhile, risking his life and liberty, Kodály spared no pains in helping those persecuted. During the siege of Budapest he sought refuge in the shelters of the Próféta utca Convent and the Opera House. It was there that he finished the *Missa Brevis,* dedicated to "my dearest wife and life companion".

143 / At the Book Fair, 1943

144 / With his wife

Not a single bridge remained intact. The Nazi troops, though surrounded, destroyed them all. The building of the Academy of Sciences and most of the houses were badly damaged and traffic was paralysed. However, there remained within the liberated people sufficient strength to find their bearings within a relatively short period of time. Kodály paid tribute to the victims of the war in his composition entitled: *By the Tomb of Martyrs*. His twelve little piano pieces entitled *Children's Dances* were written for Hungary's youth. Shortly after Hungary's liberation his *Missa Brevis* was introduced, the first performance being given in the lower cloakroom of the Opera House. Then, on March 15 the *Psalmus* was heard again, with the composer conducting. Kodály accepted the Presidency of the Hungarian Arts Council and the Free Association of Musicians. After the ordeals of the long siege Kodály rested at Pécs and Dombóvár. It was in Pécs that the sad news reached him: his true friend and comrade, Béla Bartók, had died in New York on September 26, 1945. Another old friend, Béla Balázs, returned to Hungary after twenty-six years of exile, and he immediately asked Kodály to compose the incidental music for his new drama, the *Ballad of Czinka Panna*.

146 / KODÁLY IN FRONT OF THE CATHEDRAL OF PÉCS [1945]   147 / BÉLA BALÁZS RETURNING HOME [1945]

148 / THE FIRST ART EXHIBITION IN BUDAPEST AFTER THE LIBERATION. KODÁLY IN THE COMPANY OF SCULPTOR BÉNI FERENCZY AND HIS WIFE (PHOTO BY KÁROLY ESCHER)

Life begins again. Intellectual rehabilitation was no less important than the rebuilding of bridges and houses. Kodály played an active part in this from the start. He worked even during his rest in Pécs: he began to compose the music of *Czinka Panna*, and he continued his reform of musical education with renewed energy. On Kodály's initiative the music teachers of Pécs organized the first "musical preparatory course" for aural training. His method was subsequently adopted all over the country.

149 / THE FIRST GARDEN PARTY AT THE PARK CLUB OF BUDAPEST AFTER THE LIBERATION. KODÁLY AND MRS. KODÁLY IN THE COMPANY OF ACTRESS GIZI BAJOR (PHOTO BY KÁROLY ESCHER)

In London he was received by Edward Dent, a Professor at Cambridge, and an old friend [September, 1946]

Rehearsing with the BBC Symphony Orchestra. The programme included the *Concerto* and the *Missa Brevis* [October 1946].

A reception at the Hungarian Legation in London. From left to right: Kodály, Mrs. Bede, Mrs. Kodály, Arthur Bliss, the British composer, and Mr. Bede, the Hungarian Envoy [October 1946].

Kodály arrived in New York with his wife on October 28, 1946, aboard the SS Franconia. (On the extreme left is Alfréd Márkus, the operetta composer.) By Christmas he had conducted his own compositions in eight cities. After his tiring concert tour he rested in New York in the company of Bartók's widow and his son and their mutual friends.

155 / KODÁLY WINDING UP HIS CONCERT TOUR
OF THE UNITED STATES IN CLEVELAND, OHIO,
WITH CONDUCTOR FRIGYES (FRITZ) REINER,
ON THE OCCASION OF A HIGHLY SUCCESSFUL
KODÁLY EVENING PRESENTED BY THE PITTSBURG
SYMPHONY ORCHESTRA EARLY IN JANUARY 1947.
HE SPENT FEBRUARY IN LONDON. HE CON-
DUCTED A RADIO PERFORMANCE OF HIS "MISSA
BREVIS" AND MET HIS PUBLISHER. BECAUSE OF
HITLER'S OCCUPATION OF AUSTRIA, IN 1938
KODÁLY AND BARTÓK HAD CHOSEN THE FIRM
OF BOOSEY AND HAWKES TO PUBLISH THEIR
WORKS.

156 / AFTER TALKS WITH HIS PUBLISHER. FROM LEFT TO RIGHT: WILLMETZ, BOOSEY (ONE OF THE PARTNERS
OF THE PUBLISHING FIRM OF BOOSEY AND HAWKES), KODÁLY, R. FERDINAND AND COOLUS

157 / Kodály Concert in Moscow. The programme included the "Concerto," the "Háry Suite," the "Dances from Galánta" and "The Peacock" (May 1947)

During March and April, on his way home from London, he conducted some of his works in Paris, Geneva and Lugano; then allowing himself hardly a week of rest he set off for the Soviet Union. He gave concerts in Moscow and Leningrad which were hailed as great successes, and at the Association of Composers he exchanged musical ideas with his Soviet colleagues.

158 / Kodály with his wife and Ferenc Szabó, his former composition pupil, at Leningrad Station [May 31, 1947]

159–160 / At the Hungarian Radio (Hungarian Central Newscast Photos)

Kodály talks about his eight-month concert tour in an interview with István Raics. He records a few songs from the *Czinka Panna Ballad* with László Jámbor, Lilian Birkás and Endre Rösler. Its première on November 19, 1947 was broadcast by radio stations in London and New York.

161 / Giving an account of his experiences, at the Hungarian Academy of Sciences. He was elected President of the Academy in 1946, and was responsible for the reorganization carried out during his three years of office. Beside him, the Nobel-Prize winner scientist Albert Szent-Györgyi (photo by Károly Escher)

162/ The sixty-five-year-old maestro is greeted by violin virtuoso Ede Zathureczky, Director-General of the Academy of Music. From left to right: Ernő Unger, Rezső Kókai, Kodály, Zoltán Gárdonyi, Sándor Reschofsky, Dezső Rados, Mrs. Kodály, Pál Kadosa, Zathureczky, Ferenc Szabó, Pál Járdányi, Aladár Tóth, Annie Fischer, and Gyula Ortutay (photo by Károly Falus)

163 / 1948 WAS DECLARED THE CENTENNIAL OF THE WAR OF INDEPENDENCE WAGED IN 1848 AGAINST HABSBURG OPPRESSION. KODÁLY WAS AMONG THE FIRST TO BE AWARDED THE RECENTLY ESTABLISHED KOSSUTH PRIZE. HIS NEW WORK, "CZINKA PANNA," WITH ITS TEXT BY BÉLA BALÁZS, WAS THE HIGH POINT OF THE MARCH CELEBRATIONS. ON ACCOUNT OF IDEOLOGICAL OBJECTIONS TO THE WORDS THE OPERA WAS, HOWEVER, WITHDRAWN. ITS PRECIOUS MUSIC STILL AWAITS A NEW DISCOVERER. THE CLIMAX OF THE COMPOSITION WAS THE REBIRTH OF THE "RÁKÓCZI MARCH" ON THE VIOLIN OF PANNA CZINKA. (MARGIT LUKÁCS IN THE TITLE ROLE.) (PHOTO BY PÁL M. VAJDA)

"The theatre is neither a chronicle, nor a historiography," Kodály said. "A good play does not materialize from the accumulation of even the most authentic data. A play must be more authentic than reality—it should give the illusion of reality. That is why I re-wrote the *Rákóczi March*—without trying to discover which of its motifs are contemporary or more recent. The melody slowly builds up or rather unfolds through the plucking of an amorphous melodic fragment on the violin, simultaneously with the happenings on stage."

164 / THE "PSALMUS HUNGARICUS" IS TWENTY-FIVE YEARS OLD. MRS. KODÁLY, THE SCULPTOR PÁL PÁTZAY (1896–1979) AND KODÁLY AT AN OPEN-AIR GALA CONCERT, HELD IN THE KÁROLYI GARDENS ON JULY 5, 1948

165 / Two members of
the audience at the gala
concert of the "Psal-
mus": writer Péter Ve-
res and Géza Voinovich,
General Secretary of
the Hungarian Academy
of Sciences

166 / A reunion with some of his former students [Budapest, October, 1948]. From left to right: Gyula Kertész, Kodály, Iván Engel (Switzerland), Tibor Serly (USA), Mátyás Seiber (England), István Szelényi, Jenő Ádám, Lajos Bárdos, Mihály Szigeti and György Kerényi (photo by Orelly)

99

167 / His three-year Presidency of the Hungarian Academy of Sciences ended in 1949. However, he continued to direct the Committee of Musicology and the Folk-Music Research Group which he had established. His work on musical education continued and the first volume of the "Corpus Musicae Popularis Hungaricae", "Children's Games", edited by György Kerényi, appeared in 1951

168 / Accepting an invitation to Britain he conducted a concert of his works in Glasgow at the end of 1949 and in London at the beginning of 1950

169 / With Mátyás Seiber [London, February 1950]

170 / Aboard a pleasure boat on Lake Balaton (Summer 1950)

171 / With Director-General Ede Zathureczky, who proposed that Kodály should participate in the administration of the Academy of Music as its President

172 / On a folksong collecting tour again after a long interruption. Thanks to Gyula Kertész (far left) Kodály has a tape recorder for the first time in his life (Mohács, September 1950)

173–174 / KODÁLY, LOOKING FOR SUITABLE INSTRUMENTS FOR THE MUSICAL EDUCATION OF CHILDREN, TRIES OUT A WOODEN CIMBALOM AND A RECORDER [1952] (MTI PHOTO BY KÁROLY GINK)

175–176 / ON THE THRESHOLD OF HIS 70TH YEAR KODÁLY PREPARED FOR THE PRINTERS THE FOLKSONG COLLECTION OF JÁNOS ARANY, THE GREAT HUNGARIAN POET. THE TWO PROOF-SHEETS GIVEN TO BENCE SZABOLCSI DISPLAY PHILOLOGICAL THOROUGHNESS

177 / THE PRESIDENT OF THE PRESIDENTIAL COUNCIL, SÁNDOR RÓNAI, PRESENTS THE KOSSUTH PRIZE TO KODÁLY (MTI PHOTO)

The year 1952 became virtually a Kodály year. In March the Hungarian Government awarded the 70-year-old master another Kossuth Prize, and in December the First Degree of the Order of the Hungarian People's Republic along with the title of Outstanding Artist. The Hungarian Academy of Sciences commemorated the occasion with a memorial album.

178 / AT A RECEPTION ON DECEMBER 15, HE CHATS WITH MINISTER OF CULTURE JÓZSEF RÉVAI. BEHIND THEM ARE JENŐ SZÉLL, ISTVÁN VERMES AND IMRE CSENKI (MTI PHOTO BY JENŐ PAPP)

179 / His fingers entice new harmonies from the piano (photo by Gyula Kertész)

Even during the celebrations new plans were maturing. His simple little chorus for children, the *Song of Peace* [setting of a poem by Sándor Weöres, which the chorus of the Marcibányi tér School performed for the first time on November 23, 1952, prior to Kodály's address at the Peace Congress] and his series of two- and three-part singing exercises showed that the master was turning more and more towards the young.

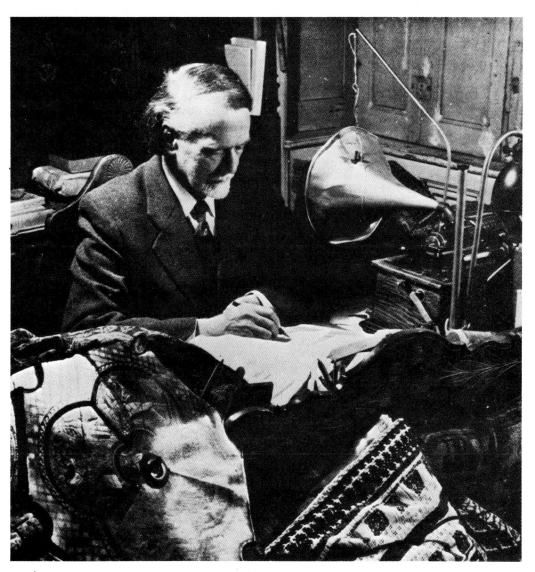

180 / CHECKING OLD TUNES AT HIS DESK USING THE OLD PHONOGRAPH (MTI PHOTO BY KÁROLY GINK)

Constant contact with folk music was a vital necessity for Kodály. His teaching was also based on this. He wanted to make young people capable of understanding classical masterpieces by training them through their own folksongs. He desired to develop both their taste and their culture so that there should never again be a musician "who does not hear what he sees, and see what he hears!"

181–182 / At home [1953] (photo by Gyula Kertész)

183 / A stroll at Galyatető [July 1954] (photo by Márton Máriaföldy)

In August 1954 his wife had an accident. She was hospitalized with a fractured femur. Kodály spent most of his time at her bedside.

184 / He also taught at the Academy of Music in the 1953–54 school-year. He had the students of musicology sing Bertalotti Solfege. Beside him is László Vikár

185 / Lesson of solmization on the lawn. Teacher—Éva Mánya; guests—Mrs. Lajos Nemesszeghy, Ede Zathureczky, Magda Szávai, Kodály, and Headmaster of Tarhos, György Gulyás

The country's first school specializing in singing and music came into existence at Békés Tarhos, in November 1946, on the initiative of György Gulyás. During its eight years of activity it trained numerous excellent musicians.

186 / The inauguration of the music building at Tarhos on May 1, 1953, built by the students and teachers. Beside Kodály is György Gulyás

187/ The first performance of "Zrínyi's Appeal", a work written for baritone and mixed chorus, at the Academy of Music (December 18, 1955). Kodály with Imre Palló and Zoltán Vásárhelyi (MTI photo by Dezső Sziklai)

The dedication of the work reads: *To my life's faithful companion, at her bedside on the occasion of our 45th anniversary.*

188–189 / He arranged the Székely folk ballad, "Mónár Anna", for voice and piano in 1924, but in 1942. provided it with a small orchestral accompaniment. The manuscript was lost, so he made another transcription of it (in 1956) with some changes. Two pages in the composer's hand

190–191 / HE FREQUENTLY CALLED AT THE HUNGARIAN ACADEMY OF SCIENCES, GUIDING AND ADVISING THE FOLK-MUSIC RESEARCH GROUP IN THEIR WORK. THE PHOTO SHOWS HIM WITH HIS CO-WORKERS PÁL JÁRDÁNYI, LAJOS KISS AND GYÖRGY KERÉNYI RESPECTIVELY [1956] (MTI PHOTO BY TAMÁS FÉNYES)

192 / SOVIET GUESTS: V. F. KUHARSKY, DEPUTY MINISTER OF CULTURE, AND COMPOSER ARAM KHACHATURIAN [SEPTEMBER 1956] (MTI PHOTO BY FERENC BARTAL)

The 75th anniversary of the birth of Béla Bartók was celebrated in Budapest with an international conference and a series of concerts. The chairman of the Memorial Committee was Zoltán Kodály.

193 / THE OPENING OF THE BARTÓK CELEBRATIONS ON SEPTEMBER 26, 1956. BESIDE KODÁLY IS COMPOSER FERENC SZABÓ AND THE WRITER JÓZSEF DARVAS, MINISTER OF CULTURE (MTI PHOTO BY ANDOR TORMAI)

194 / The Pathé-Marconi Company made a new recording of the "Psalmus Hungaricus". The composer conducted the Hungarian State Symphony Orchestra and the Budapest Chorus. The soloist was Endre Rösler [March 6, 1957] (MTI photo by Dezső Sziklai)

Mrs. Kodály's improving health permitted them to spend a few months at Galyatető, but in January 1957 his commitments summoned him to Budapest once again.

195 / Consultation during a break in the recording session. Kodály with conductor Miklós Forrai and Endre Rösler (MTI photo by Dezső Sziklai)

196 / Kodálv was awarded the Kossuth Prize for the third time. With István Dobi, President of the Presidential Council, and Gyula Kállai at the presentation [March 1957] [MTI photo]

197 / Celebration in Debrecen. Kodály speaks at the inauguration of the music school named after him. Beside him is János Ménes, Council President, and Headmaster György Gulyás, who continued his activities here after the cessation of the school at Békés Tarhos (June, 1957)

198 / A weekday in Debrecen. Kodály, accompanied by György Gulyás and Pál Járdányi, visits a solfège class at the Music Secondary School to see whether "it was able to set an example in the coordination of instruction in solfège and instrument playing," as he expected of such schools (Artistic Coop. photo)

After more than three decades of struggle, through the enthusiastic work of Kodály's pupils and followers and through the effective support of the State, his ideas began to turn into a living, active force. Already more than 70 primary schools in the country were providing six hours of singing instruction per week—the first among them having been the school of Mrs. Lajos Nemesszeghy at Kecskemét. Again musical training in the kindergarten acquired prominence. Kodály once again published his paper entitled *Music in the Kindergarten,* enlarged with a postscript. He assisted Katalin Forrai's pioneering venture.

199 / At the Csobánc utca Musical Kindergarten's "examination". Katalin Forrai's class [Budapest, June, 1957] (photo by László Vikár)

200 / At the General Assembly of the Eötvös Loránd University of Arts and Sciences in December 1957 with Rector Gyula Ortutay (MTI photo by Andor Tormai)

The Budapest University conferred an honorary doctor's degree on the 75-year-old master, the Hungarian Academy of Sciences honoured him with a memorial album, and the Belgian Academy of Sciences elected him a member. The musical community greeted him with festive programmes and concerts.

201 / With singer Erzsi Török, a well-known performer of folk music and of Kodály's songs, and Gyula Ortutay, during the intermission of one of the concerts [Budapest, December 1957] (photo by László Vámos)

202 / Yehudi Menuhin with the Kodálys in their home (photo by István Harmath)

203 / In the hills of Buda

204 / A new score appeared entitled "Variations for the Piano" composed by Mrs. Zoltán Kodály (photo by Gyula Kertész)

Some of the last photographs of the Kodálys together. Emma Kodály died on November 22, 1958 after forty-nine years of marriage.

205 / ALONE... WINTER IN THE MÁTRA HILLS [GALYATETŐ, JANUARY 1959] (PHOTO BY GYÖRGY SZOMJAS SCHIFFERT)

Kodály's farewell to his wife: "During her life she was a blessing to all those who met her. Wherever she turned, her look engendered light, warmth and life, for her bright eyes reflected infinite kindness. All those who have experienced even a small part of the affection and warmth she radiated will feel sadly bereaved. But most grievously bereaved is the man on whom she lavished most, whose life she made a paradise on earth." As a composer, Kodály bade Emma farewell by writing the funeral chorus *I Will Go Look for Death* the setting of a poem by John Masefield.

116

206 / THE HAYDN COMMEMORATIVE SESSION AT THE ACADEMY OF SCIENCES. VILMOS TÁTRAI PLAYED THE VIOLIN AND BENCE SZABOLCSI THE PIANO. ZOLTÁN KODÁLY TURNED THE PAGES [FEBRUARY 1959] (MTI PHOTO BY EDIT MOLNÁR)

207 / A CHAT AFTER THE FIRST PERFORMANCE OF THE CHORUS "HONEY, HONEY, HONEY," AT THE SZILÁGYI ERZSÉBET SECONDARY SCHOOL FOR GIRLS [APRIL, 1959]

208 / WITH VIOLINIST DAVID OISTRAKH AT THE LATTER'S BUDAPEST CONCERT [MARCH 1959] (PHOTO BY ISTVÁN HARMATH)

117

209 / With István Rusz-
nyák and László Orbán
at the opening of the
Hungarian Academy `of
Sciences' International
Haydn Conference in
September 1959 (MTI
photo by Edit Molnár)

210 / An autumn stroll in the Buda hills with an old friend Emil Telmányi, and his family. At the front are: Kodály, Telmányi, Sarolta Péczely and Mrs. Telmányi. Behind them are Telmányi's daughters, both concert violinists [1959] (photo by Emil Telmányi)

211 / THE FOLK-MUSIC RESEARCH GROUP SAW KODÁLY OFF AT BUDAPEST AIRPORT ON APRIL 29, 1960, WHEN HE LEFT FOR A SIX-WEEK TOUR OF ENGLAND. FROM LEFT TO RIGHT: LAJOS KISS, PÁL JÁRDÁNYI, GÉZA PAULOVITS, IMRE OLSVAI (HIDDEN), LÁSZLÓ VIKÁR, BENJAMIN RAJECZKY, MÁTÉ PÁL, GYÖRGY KERÉNYI AND KODÁLY

After a year in mourning Zoltán Kodály married Sarolta Péczely, the daughter of old friends, on December 18, 1959. At the time she was studying singing and choral conducting at the Academy of Music. She decided to give up her chosen career because she regarded her new calling to be of greater importance. She brought solace and joy to Kodály's life, put an end to his solitude, and even resolved his proverbial taciturnity.

212 / OXFORD UNIVERSITY CONFERRED AN HONORARY DEGREE ON KODÁLY, ON MAY 3, 1960, ON WHICH OCCASION HE DELIVERED A LECTURE ENTITLED "FOLK MUSIC AND ART MUSIC". SUBSEQUENTLY CONCERTS OF HIS WORKS WERE GIVEN IN BIRMINGHAM AND LONDON. IT WAS AROUND THIS TIME THAT SIR ARTHUR BLISS SAID: "KODÁLY'S VOICE IN MUSIC IS THE VOICE OF HUNGARY"

213 / THE DEUTSCHE GRAMOPHON RECORDING COMPANY COMMISSIONED A STEREO RECORDING OF THE "CONCERTO". THE COMPOSER HIMSELF CONDUCTED [BUDAPEST, JULY 1960] (MTI PHOTO BY ENDRE FRIEDMANN)

214 / KODÁLY GAVE A LECTURE ON ENGLISH VOCAL MUSIC AT THE BRITISH EMBASSY, BUDAPEST, IN NOVEMBER 1960. AT THE RECEPTION AFTER THE LECTURE HE CHATTED WITH ANTAL MOLNÁR. BESIDE THEM: JÁNOS VISKI, ISTVÁN KAPITÁNFFY AND MRS. SAROLTA KODÁLY (PHOTO BY ISTVÁN HARMATH)

215 / KODÁLY, ON THE WAY TO RECOVERY AFTER A HEART ATTACK WATCHES THE PLAYING OF A MISKOLC FOLK ARTIST, RUDOLF VÉKONY BURI [APRIL 1961] (PHOTO BY GYULA KERTÉSZ)

216–217 / YEHUDI MENUHIN VISITED KODÁLY ON JUNE 23, 1961, NOT JUST AS A FRIEND, BUT ALSO AS A MUSICIAN WHO HAD BEEN WAITING FOR YEARS FOR KODÁLY TO WRITE A VIOLIN CONCERTO. KODÁLY GAVE HIM THE SCORE OF THE RECENTLY FINISHED "SYMPHONY," WHICH HE TOOK TO FERENC FRICSAY, THE CONDUCTOR WHO PREMIERED IT (PHOTO BY ISTVÁN HARMATH)

218 / On August 16, 1961, the Swiss Festival Orchestra, conducted by Ferenc Fricsay, gave the "Symphony" its first performance in Lucerne. The three-movement work is dedicated to the memory of Toscanini. Its use of folk music, tonal principles and classical structure reflect the whole of Kodály's life's work. Over a period of eighteen months the "Symphony" was presented in about fifty cities

219 / With cellist Pierre Fournier soon after the première of the "Symphony"

220 / A boat trip on Lake Vierwaldstätt in August 1961

122

221 / On the occasion of the 80th anniversary of Bartók's birth, a conference on musicology was held in September 1961. Mrs. Kodály, Mrs. Ditta Bartók-Pásztory and Kodály during the recess

222–223 / On Kodály's 79th birthday Ilona Andor's girls choir, the first to adopt the composer's name, gave a concert in his honour. István Péterfy, the music critic and old comrade, cordially greeted Kodály [Budapest, December 18, 1961]

224 / A MEMBER OF THE JURY AT THE INTERNATIONAL COMPETITION FOR COMPOSERS IN BRUSSELS [NOVEMBER 1961] (PHOTO BY CHARLES LEIRENS)

225 / WITH PIANIST SVIATOSLAV RICHTER AT THE LATTER'S BUDAPEST CONCERT [SEPTEMBER 27, 1961] (MTI PHOTO BY EDIT MOLNÁR)

226 / Laying the founda-
tion-stone of the Cul-
tural Centre in the vil-
lage of Dunapataj, June
10, 1962 (photo by Toro-
nyi)

"This is the only foun-
dation-stone I was asked
to lay in the material
sense of the word. For
a long time, however, I
have been doing nothing
else but laying intellectual foundation-stones. I
feel like the farmer who,
according to an ancient
Latin proverb, planted
trees but realized that
he himself would never
enjoy their fruits."

227 / Two weeks later
in Rome he received the
Gold Medal of the
Academy St. Cecilia
(photo by Franco
P. Caudarella)

125

229–230 / Kodály's visitors are conductor Roberto Benzi and the Solisti Veneti chamber-music ensemble (photo by István Harmath)

231–232 / A CELEBRATION AT KECSKEMÉT, KODÁLY'S BIRTHPLACE. ON THE MORNING OF DECEMBER 16, 1962 THE EIGHTY-YEAR-OLD COMPOSER UNVEILS A STATUE OF KECSKEMÉT'S OTHER GREAT SON, THE DRAMATIST JÓZSEF KATONA (1791–1830). ON KODÁLY'S LEFT IS THE POET GYULA ILLYÉS (MTI PHOTO BY EDIT MOLNÁR)
IN THE EVENING, AT THE KATONA JÓZSEF THEATRE, ILLYÉS HONOURS THE MASTER WITH A POEM ENTITLED: "INTRODUCTION TO A KODÁLY CONCERT". SEATED IN THE BOX ARE MRS. KODÁLY, MRS. ILLYÉS, KODÁLY AND COUNCIL CHAIRMAN GÉZA REILE (PHOTO BY LÁSZLÓ VÁMOS)

233–234 / The octogenerian composer... as painter József Szalatnyai and photographer László Vámos saw him

128

235 / The Hungarian Academy of Sciences held a session and issued a newer memorial album in Kodály's honour. Ferenc Erdei, the General Secretary, praised the celebrated composer (photo by László Vámos)

236 / The most interesting gift was the "Salutation" of Kodály's former pupils: a series of variations for orchestra on one of his themes. The works of the five former pupils living abroad were broadcast by the Vienna Radio, and those of the composers residing in Hungary were presented by the Budapest Radio. The latter were heard by Kodály—together with his pupils—in the studio (photo by László Vámos)

237 / In the Munkácsy Hall of Parliament, István Dobi, President of the Presidential Council (on his left is János Kádár) conferred upon the 80-year-old master the highest degree of the Order of the Hungarian People's Republic. Below the painting: Tibor Sárai, Ferenc Szabó, István Rusznyák and Kálmán Nádasdy (MTI photo by Ferenc Vigovszki)

238 / At the Association of Hungarian Musicians, György Aczél, the First Deputy Minister of Culture, Ferenc Szabó and Tibor Sárai greet Kodály (photo by László Vámos)

131

At the Academy of Music he acknowledges the applause of the audience with Miklós Lukács, Miklós Forrai and Róbert Ilosfalvy (photo by László Vámos)

A chat during an intermission with Bence Szabolcsi, Aladár Tóth and Ferenc Szabó (photo by István Harmath)

In the company of sculptor Zsigmond Kisfaludi Strobl, Minister of Culture Pál Ilku and Ferenc Szabó (photo by István Harmath)

242 / Kodály, in the happy atmosphere of his home, working on new compositions (MTI photo by Edit Molnár)

243 / At the Sixth Hungarian Peace Congress with Pál Ilku [Budapest, June 1963] (MTI photo by Gábor Pálfai)

Kodály, feeling a sense of responsibility for his people, contributed to the social struggle for progress and the preservation of peace not only with his choruses and his educational activities, but also by speaking in public.

244 / In August 1963, The International Folk Music Council (IFMC) held its conference in Jerusalem. Kodály—President of the Council since 1961—gave the introductory lecture under the title, "East and West in Music" (photo by W. Braun). He attends the première of "The Spinning Room" in Hebrew

245 / An excursion to Capernaum after the conference

246 / With József Szigeti. The famous violinist was in Budapest in the autumn of 1963 as the honorary President of the Bartók–Weiner Festival. Kodály wrote the preface to the Hungarian edition of Szigeti's memoirs (MTI photo by Edit Molnár)

In October 1963, in the company of Ferenc Szabó, he attended the Music Education Conference at Coppenhagen. His educational concept aroused great interest in Danish music teaching circles

247 / On an excursion to Kronborg with his wife and Ferenc Szabó after the conference

248 / A meeting in Lenin-
grad with a group of
Soviet-Georgian com-
posers. From left to
right: Balanchivadze,
Jorjiashvili, Toradze,
Nasidze, Lobkovsky,
Tsintsadze

249 / In front of the Hermitage in Leningrad, December 1963

250 / A Kodály Gala Concert in the auditorium of the Moscow Conservatoire on December 19, 1963. The "Psalmus", the "Háry Suite" and the "Symphony" were conducted by Constantin Ivanov

251 / The first performance of "Háry János" in Russian, in Moscow, on December 21, 1963, with Kemal Abdullayev conducting

252 / Tikhon Khrenikov on behalf of the Association of Soviet Composers greeted Kodály who was elected an honorary professor of the Moscow Conservatoire [December 1963] (MTI photo)

253 / The Humboldt University of Berlin, which Kodály attended as a student in 1906–1907, conferred an honorary doctor's degree on him in 1964. Here he is with the Rector, Dr. Schroeder (photo by MTI)

His wide international acclaim came not only as a result of his artistic and musicological efforts, but also because of his humanitarian views.

254 / The inauguration of the new building of the "Kodály Zoltán" Primary and Secondary School of Singing and Music in Kecskemét in February 1964. On the left of Kodály are Zoltán Vásárhelyi and Mrs. Nemesszeghy, Márta Szentkirályi, the founder and Director of the school (MTI photo by Attila Lajos)

This was the first school in the country to integrate musical education into the general academic curriculum. Mrs. Nemesszeghy began it in the autumn of 1950 with a single class in a rented classroom, taking as a model the school at Békés Tarhos. With inexhaustible energy and real determination she established the type of school which Kodály had envisaged: *Let our schools embarking on new roads find all the more followers.*

255 / Zoltán name-day greetings in the Folk Music Research Group: the Kodálys and Benjamin Rajeczky listen to the singing of Andrea Zsadon, Adrienne Csengery and Judit Várbíró [March 8, 1964] (photo by Rudolf Vigh)

256 / A LETTER TO HIS OLD FRIEND AND COLLEAGUE ANTAL MOLNÁR FROM GALYATETŐ IN WHICH HE DISCUSSES THE EFFECTIVENESS OF RADIO LECTURES AND PROPOSES TO LAY OUT NEW APPROACHES TO MUSICAL EDUCATION. THE POSTCARD WAS AN INVITATION AND AT THE SAME TIME A REMINISCENCE. "IT'S GOOD TO BE HERE AGAIN, BUT I WOULD HAPPILY GIVE THIS HOTEL IN EXCHANGE FOR THE LEAKING LOG-CABIN IN WHICH I SPENT A NIGHT SIXTY YEARS OR SO AGO, WHEN I FIRST VISITED THESE PARTS. ...THAT WAS THE ONLY 'BUILDING' HERE FOR MILES AROUND".

258 / TWO MONTHS LATER THE INTERNATIONAL FOLK MUSIC COUNCIL ALSO HELD ITS CONFERENCE IN BUDAPEST. A TELEVISION INTERVIEW WITH MEMBERS OF THE STANDING COMMITTEE. FROM LEFT TO RIGHT: W. RHODES, W. M. BELYAYEV, REPORTER JÁNOS SEBESTYÉN, KODÁLY AND PÁL JÁRDÁNYI (MTI PHOTO BY EDIT MOLNÁR)

257 / In June 1964, the International Society of Musical Education (ISME) held its conference in Budapest. Minister of Education Pál Ilku welcomes Kodály, Honorary President of the Conference. The five hundred delegates recommended that the member countries of the Society establish music schools similar to those set up throughout Hungary (MTI photo by Edit Molnár)

259 / DURING AN INTERMISSION AT THE CONFERENCE. FROM LEFT TO RIGHT: MARGIT TÓTH, FOLK-MUSIC RESEARCHER, PÁL ILKU, BÉLA BARTÓK JR. AND KODÁLY (PHOTO BY LÁSZLÓ KEMÉNY)

260 / AT THE FOLK MUSIC CONFERENCE: KODÁLY IS SEEN HERE WITH A YOUNG FOLK ENSEMBLE AND ITS LEADER, MRS. VANKÓ, WHO UNDER HER MAIDEN NAME, JULI DUDÁS, IS A FAMOUS FOLK PAINTER OF GALGAMÁCSA (PHOTO BY LÁSZLÓ KEMÉNY)

261 / THE CONFERENCE VISITED KECSKEMÉT: KODÁLY, MRS. NEMESSZEGHY AND MAUD KARPELES, THE HONORARY PRESIDENT OF THE COUNCIL, IN THE FOYER OF THE NEW SCHOOL [AUGUST 23, 1964]

At the conference many delegates were amazed by the fact that in Hungarian music primary schools children of average ability learn to read music and sightsing between the ages of eight and ten.

Guests of Budapest's musical life are also Kodály's guests.

262 / With Benjamin Britten [1964] (MTI photo by Edit Molnár)

263 / With Pablo Casals [1964] (photo by István Harmath)

264 / The Helikon festivities at Keszt-
hely, May 1965. Kodály delivers an
address and the youth choruses of Pécs
perform his new choral work entitled
"Mohács"

265 / At the general assembly of the
Hungarian Academy of Sciences with
his old friend, the linguist Dezső Pais
[April 1965] (MTI photo by Ferenc
Vigovszki)

Kodály's major concern was the musical education of young people. He always found time to visit schools and to listen to young people's choirs.

267 / The choir of the Szilágyi Erzsébet Girls' High School, Budapest, gives a concert in Kodály's honour. The Szilágyi Choir was already famous in the 20s, when it was led by Adrienne Sztojanovits (sitting at Kodály's left in the picture). Toscanini had praised the achievements of the choir, while Kodály commemorated its high standards by the dedication of "Whitsuntide" (photo by László Vámos)

268 / THE RECTOR OF THE UNIVERSITY OF VIENNA AWARDING KODÁLY THE HERDER PRIZE, IN APRIL 1965, IN RECOGNITION OF HIS ACTIVITIES IN THE FURTHERANCE OF EAST–WEST CULTURAL RELATIONS. BEHIND HIM, LÁSZLÓ NÉMETH, THE HUNGARIAN WRITER WHO WAS ALSO AWARDED THE PRIZE

At the same time as the festivities in Vienna, *The Spinning Room* was given its first full performance in Paris (in a concert performance).

269 / WITH AUSTRIAN CHANCELLOR DR. JOSEF KLAUS, AT THE FIRST SHOWING OF THE FILM HÁRY JÁNOS, IN THE COLLEGIUM HUNGARICUM, VIENNA, APRIL 1965 (PHOTO BY OSCAR HOROWITZ)

270/ Visiting Eugene Or-
mándy, conductor of
the Philadelphia Or-
chestra and an excel-
lent interpreter of his
works

In June Kodály was Britten's guest at the Aldeburgh Festival where he heard the first performance of Britten's new work, the Gemini Variations (the theme being Kodály's). He then left for the United States. At the invitation of the Ford Foundation he studied the methods used in the education of musicians at several universities. In Hanover conductor Bonaventura devoted four concerts to his works.

271 / The "Te Deum" was a great success at the "Kodály Festival" in Dartmouth College, Hanover, New Hampshire (USA). Kodály with conductor Mario di Bonaventura and singers Gwendolyn Walters and Caroline Stanford [August 1, 1965] (photo by Heinz Kluetmeier)

272–273 / "I WAS BORN IN KECSKEMÉT…" REMINISCENCES WRITTEN BY KODÁLY AT THE REQUEST OF THE AUTHOR OF THE PRESENT VOLUME [1965]

In spite of the range of his literary activity, statements of an autobiographical nature scarcely amount to more than a few pages. When I called his attention to this circumstance, requesting him to write about his compositions and about himself, he was non-committal for a long time, saying: "Every composer writes his own autobiography with his scores. You only have to read them to get a better and truer insight into his life than you will from any autobiography. But you have to understand the language of music…" Nevertheless, the reminiscences (printed in facsimile here) may have served as the introduction to a planned but never realized autobiography.

"There was always in me a hankering after mountains," he wrote, "but I was not able to satisfy it for a long time. From Galánta, I saw the chain of the Little Carpathians looming in the distance. From Nagyszombat they looked much nearer, but I did not get the chance to climb them until years later. At that time it was not the custom to hike or go on excursions… It was a grave omission in the educational policy of the period that it never encouraged the young to wander round their country. My fellow students knew nothing of Hungary outside their immediate neighbourhood. Father worked on the railways and took me and my younger brother along on his summer trips. We saw the valley of the Vág, Kassa, Kolozsvár, Brassó and Budapest at the time of the Millennium. While spending a summer with relatives at Resicza I got an inkling of what real mountains were. But I did not become a 'mountaineer' until later."

275 / WITH COMPOSER DMITRI SHOSTAKOVICH AT THE BUDAPEST PREMIÈRE OF HIS OPERA KATERINA IZMAYLOVA ▷ [DECEMBER 1965] (MTI PHOTO BY EDIT MOLNÁR)

274 / With Menuhin and conductor János Ferencsik at the season's opening concert in Budapest [September 1964]
(MTI photo by Edit Molnár)

Kodály was very pedantic and circumspect even in publishing matters. He gave voice to his desires in a very decisive manner: "It is untenable that no piano scores of the *Psalmus* are printed with Hungarian text. Since the rhythm is adapted to the translations, it cannot be used for Hungarian words. Performances in the original language are not rare even abroad (Geneva, Moscow, France, Holland), but copies are also needed in Hungary."

277 / BIRTHDAY GREETINGS TO SCHLEE: VARIATIONS ON THE INITIALS OF HIS NAME, COMPOSED IN THE OLD VIENNESE STYLE (FIRST FACSIMILE EDITION OF PAGE 1 OF THE MANUSCRIPT)

278 / In Paris at the 20th Congress of the International Association of Jeunesses Musicales he delivered a lecture in French on the advantages of a musical education which is based on singing [April 1966] (photo by Károly Forgács)

279 / On a lecture tour of the United States he spoke about his approach to musical education at universities in Stanford, Ann Arbor and Santa Barbara.— The Kodálys with pianist Ernő Dániel and composer Richard Johnston [July 1966]

280 / Toronto, July 7, 1966: The 140-year-old University of Toronto conferred an honorary degree on Kodály (photo by Jack Marshall and Co. Ltd.). Three years earlier the American Academy of Arts and Sciences had elected him an honorary member. These honours bestowed upon him showed the ever-growing interest in his life and art

281 / THE INTERNATIONAL SOCIETY OF MUSICAL EDUCATION HELD ITS 1966 CONFERENCE AT INTERLOCHEN (USA). IN A LECTURE HEARD BY DELEGATES FROM 41 COUNTRIES, KODÁLY ANALYSED THE ROLE OF THE FOLKSONG IN MUSICAL EDUCATION. "EDUCATING CHILDREN TO LOVE MUSIC CAN ONLY BE ACHIEVED BY THEIR EXPERIENCE OF MUSIC. SCHOOLS MUST UNDERTAKE TO PROVIDE THIS EXPERIENCE."

282 / At Stanford University, California (USA). The lectures delivered here by Erzsébet Szőnyi and Zoltán Kodály won many supporters for the Hungarian method of musical education. Beside them is Professor W. Kuhn [July 1966]

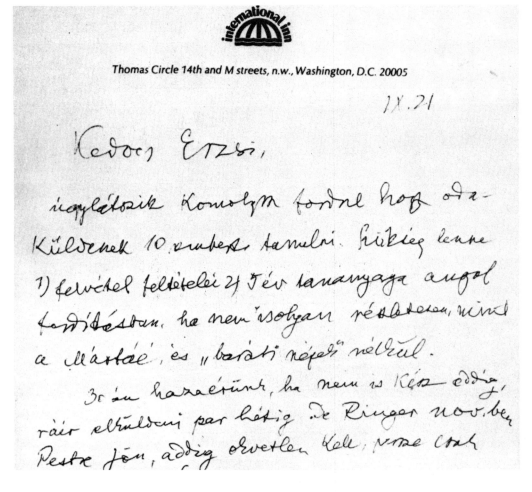

Thomas Circle 14th and M streets, n.w., Washington, D.C. 20005

283 / In September 1966 Kodály met with representatives of the Arts Council of the United States. The Council had decided to provide scholarships to enable music graduates to study the methods of teaching singing in Hungary. Kodály informed Erzsébet Szőnyi of this in a letter written in Washington: "It seems to be almost certain that ten people will be sent to Hungary to study. What would be needed now are, 1) the terms of admission and 2) an English translation of the course of study of five years..."

284 / On his way home from America, in September 1966, in the company of his former pupil, composer Géza Frid, he visited the Dutch Donemus Foundation. On his right André Jurres, Director of the Donemus (photo by Harry van Steenis)

285 / One of his last visits abroad was to see his dear old pupil Géza Frid in Holland.—In Frid's Amsterdam home with Frid's wife and composer Frank Martin [September 1966] (photo by Géza Frid)

286 / AT A PEASANT WED-
DING IN CSOMÁD, A VIL-
LAGE IN PEST COUNTY
[NOVEMBER 1966]

The idea of a new chorus was maturing in him. The chosen poem is almost like a motto:

    For God is Truth and Life,
    His command, that all shall live,
    His command, that all rejoice.

        (Endre Ady: God's Trumpet)

287 / HIS LAST BIRTHDAY
GIFT: THE MEMORABLE PER-
FORMANCE OF THE "TE
DEUM" ON DECEMBER 16,
1966. KODÁLY WITH THE
PERFORMING ARTISTS: ÉVA
ANDOR AND ERZSÉBET
KOMLÓSSY, SOLOISTS; ER-
VIN LUKÁCS, CONDUCTOR;
AND MIKLÓS FORRAI, CHO-
RAL DIRECTOR (PHOTO BY
ISTVÁN HARMATH)

288 / ONE OF HIS LAST VISITORS: CONDUCTOR
LEOPOLD STOKOWSKI, A DISCERNING INTER-
PRETER OF HIS WORKS [JANUARY 24, 1967]
(MTI PHOTO BY EDIT MOLNÁR)

289 / HIS LAST DECORATION: THE COM-
MANDER'S ORDER OF THE WHITE ROSE OF
FINLAND WAS HANDED OVER TO HIM BY
AMBASSADOR OLAVI RAUSTILA. BEHIND
KODÁLY ARE JÓZSEF BOGNÁR, PRESIDENT
OF THE INSTITUTE OF CULTURAL RELATIONS
AND GYÖRGY ACZÉL, THE FIRST DEPUTY
MINISTER OF CULTURE, AND ON HIS LEFT
IS COMPOSER PÁL KADOSA, PRESIDENT OF
THE ASSOCIATION OF MUSICIANS [FEBRUARY
17, 1967] (MTI PHOTO BY FERENC
VIGOVSZKI)

290–291 / In his home (photo by László Vámos and Gyula Kertész)

292–293 / Among the musicians of the future (photo by István Harmath)

Two sources of happiness in his last years were his home life and his meetings with children. Antal Molnár said: "Verdi was also active in his old age, but he would not have been as willing to involve himself in educating the masses. What is unique about Kodály is his complete disregard of the individual when it is a question of the common interest."

294–295 / In front of his home

296 / At the "Lorántffy Zsuzsanna" Music Primary School (photo by László Vámos)

"I devoted a great deal of time to writing choruses for children and to compiling singing books for schools. I think I shall never regret the time I lost in this way even though it could have been used for the writing of greater works. I feel I have thereby accomplished just as useful work for the common good as if I had written further symphonic compositions." (Kodály: *The Popularization of Serious Music*, 1946)

In Hungary singing is already taught in one hundred and ten primary schools every day. "This is the right way for a socialist country. I am convinced that in time all of our schools will do the same." (Kodály: A statement to the newspaper *Petőfi Népe*, 1967)

297–298 / On the Fishermen's Bastion (photos by László Vámos). Wherever he goes he is surrounded by children

299 / But he gives his autograph only to those who can solmizate (photo by István Harmath)

"We fought for these schools for many years, without even thinking of other countries. We were led only by our desire to improve our musical education system... We would be happy if our efforts and experiences proved useful to others, and especially if they helped us advance, even if only by a small step, towards mankind's common goal, the brotherhood of peoples." (Kodály: *Musical Instruction and Education,* 1966)

This was his last message. Its basic theme, and even its mode of expression obviously allude to Bartók's famous statement: "My own guiding principle... is the brotherhood of peoples." (1931) Kodály paid a last tribute to their deep and lasting friendship.

300 / The "77 Two-Part Exercises," the "Ode" for mixed choir and orchestra and the "Laudes Organi" for mixed choir and organ were completed (photo by Roger Graef)

301 / The planned new setting to music of a poem by Endre Ady, God's Trumpet —as well as the violin concerto promised to Yehudi Menuhin—were unrealized (photo by László Vámos)

302 / THE LAST FLOWERS, THE LAST PHOTOGRAPH OF KODÁLY (TAKEN BY MRS. ZOLTÁN KODÁLY ON MARCH 3, 1967)

On 27 February he went to the hospital for a check-up. He died of a heart attack on the morning of 6 March 1967. On March 11 the compassion of the many thousands of people who came to his funeral, as well as of whole nations and of the whole musical world, followed him to his final resting place.

"There can be no productive Hungarian composer who has not assimilated our Hungarian musical tradition, who has not made it blossom out of his heart and continued it in his own way. Nor can there be a productive musicologist who does not have the same living tradition seething in his blood..." (Kodály: *Ethnography and Music History,* 1933)
The basis of Kodály's art and activities was Hungarian folk music. This is the reason why his life's work was also of universal value, and is part of the treasury of all mankind.

304 / THE VOLUMES OF THE CORPUS MUSICAE POPULARIS HUNGARICAE THAT APPEARED DURING HIS LIFE

"Music increases the beauty of life and all that is precious in it."
(Kodály: Speech made at the inauguration of the new building of the Kecskemét School, 1964.)

KODÁLY'S CONTEMPORARIES IN PICTURES

An index of recognizable or identifiable persons in the pictures. Beside the names are the *picture numbers*.

Aczél, György 238, 289
Ádám, Jenő 90, 121, 166
Andor, Éva 287
Andor, Ilona 222, 223
Ansermet, Ernest 139
Antal, György 141
Atkins, Ivor 104
Bajor, Gizi 149
Balanchivadze, Andrei M. 248
Balázs, Béla 35, 147
Balogh (?) 31
Bárdos, Lajos 90, 134, 166
Bartal (?) 31
Bartók, Béla 26, 39, 44, 48, 54, 55, 64, 65, 66, 80, 83, 130
Bartók, Béla jr. 259
Bartók, Mrs. Béla, the elder 80
Bartók, Mrs. Béla, Ditta Pásztory 221
Bede, Hungarian Envoy 152
Belyayev, Victor M. 258
Benzi, Roberto 229
Birta (Bartha), László 31
Bliss, Arthur 152
Bodnár, Gyula 31
Bognár, József 289
Bonaventura, Mario di 271
Boosey (?) 156
Boreczky, Elemér 31
Britten, Benjamin 262
Bușiția, Ioan 83
Casals, Pablo 263
Coolus, 156
Czógler, Kálmán 31
Csengery, Adrienne 255
Csenki, Imre 158, 178
Csépke (?) 31
Dániel, Ernő 279
Darvas, József 191
Demeter, Béla 31
Dent, Edward 150
Dobi, István 194, 237
Dohnányi, Ernő 28, 79
Doráti, Antal 90
Draganau, Miklós 31
Engel, Iván 166
Erdei, Ferenc 235
Failoni, Sergio 118
Farkas, Ferenc 236
Ferdinand, Roger 156
Ferencsik, János 130, 274
Ferenczy, Béni 148
Fischer, Annie 162, 228
Forrai, Katalin 199
Forrai, Miklós 195, 239, 287
Fournier, Pierre 219

Fricsay, Ferenc 218
Frid, Géza 91, 284
Furtwängler, Wilhelm 140
Gárdonyi, Zoltán 162, 236
Gerevich, Tibor 31
Gianicelli, Károly 33
Gombocz, Endre 31
Gréb (?) 31
Gruber, Mrs. Henrik see Mrs. Zoltán Kodály, Emma Sándor
Gruenberg, Louis 93
Gulovics (?) 31
Gulyás, György 185, 186, 197, 198
Hajnóczy, Iván 31
Hanák, József 91
Hermann, Pál 91
Hertzka, Emil 92
Herzfeld, Viktor 25
Horusitzky, Zoltán 121
Ilku, Pál 241, 243, 257, 259
Illyés, Gyula 231
Illyés, Mrs. Gyula 232
Ilosfalvy, Róbert 239
Jakucs, István 31
Jaloveczky, Béla 74
Jaloveczky, Kornél 74
Jaloveczky, Viktor 81
Jámbor, László 160
Járdányi, Pál 162, 190, 198, 211, 258
Jatzkó, Vilmos 142
Johnston, Richard 279
Jorjiashvili, 248
Jurres, André 284
Kádár, János 237
Kadosa, Pál 162, 236, 250, 289
Kállai, Gyula 196
Kálmán, Imre 33
Kálmán, Oszkár 121
Kalocsay, Endre 31
Kapitánffy, István 214
Karpeles, Maud 261
Karvaly, Viktor 121
Kelen, Hugó 138
Kerényi, György 90, 121, 166, 191, 211
Kerpely, Jenő 48
Kertész, Gyula 90, 166, 172
Khachaturian, Aram 192
Khrenikov, Tikhon 252
Kisfaludi Strobl, Zsigmond 241
Kiss, Lajos 191, 211
Klaus, Josef 269
Kodály, Emilia 8, 12
Kodály, Frigyes 4
Kodály, Mrs. Frigyes 3, 81
Kodály, Pál 8, 12

Kodály, Mrs. Zoltán, Sarolta Péczely 210, 214, 216, 219, 220, 221, 227, 232, 236, 242, 245, 247, 249, 254, 255, 267, 278, 279, 285, 286, 290, 291, 297, 298
Kodály, Mrs. Zoltán, Emma Sándor 39, 49, 54, 55, 80, 106, 129, 144, 149, 152, 154, 158, 162, 164, 181, 182, 183, 202, 203, 204
Koessler, Hans 24
Kókai, Rezső 162
Komlóssy, Erzsébet 287
Krausz, Vilmos 31
Kuharsky, V. F. 192
Kuhn, Wolfgang 282
Lajtha, László 46
Lobkovsky, 248
Lukács, Ervin 287
Lukács, Miklós 239
Mánya, Éva 185
Márkus, Alfréd 154
Maros, Rudolf 236
Maróthy (?) 31
Martin, Frank 285
Ménes, János 197
Menuhin, Yehudi 202, 216, 217, 274
Mihalovich, Ödön 23
Molnár, Antal 34, 45, 48, 214
Nádasdy, Kálmán 237
Nasidze, 248
Nemesszeghy, Mrs. Lajos, Márta Szentkirályi 185, 254, 261
Németh, Gábor 31
Németh, László 268
Oistrakh, David 208
Olsvai, Imre 211
Orbán, László 209
Ormándy, Jenő 270
Ortutay, Gyula 162, 200, 201
Pais, Dezső 265
Pál, Máté 211
Palló, Imre 118, 121, 137, 187
Pátzay, Pál 164
Paulini, Béla 123
Paulovits, Géza 209
Péterfi, István 223
Pongrácz, Zoltán 236
Rados, Dezső 162
Rajeczky, Benjamin 211, 255
Ránki, György 236
Raustila, Erdem Olavi 289
Reile, Géza 232
Reiner, Frigyes 155
Reinitz, Béla 82
Reschofsky, Sándor 162

Révai, József 178
Rhodes, Willard 258
Richter, Sviatoslav 225
Ringbauer, Károly 31
Rónai, Sándor 177
Rösler, Endre 138, 194, 195
Rusznyák, István 209, 237
Sárai, Tibor 237, 238, 250
Scharbert, Vilmos 31
Schroeder, Dr. (Rector) 253
Sebestyén, János 258
Seiber, Mátyás 90, 166, 169
Serly, Tibor 91, 166
Shostakovich, Dmitri 275
Stanford, Caroline 271
Stockinger, László 31
Stokowski, Leopold 288
Stutschewsky, Joachim 93
Sugár, Rezső 236
Sulyok, Imre 236
Szabó, Ferenc 158, 162, 193, 236,
    237, 238, 240, 241, 247

Szabó, Miklós 31
Szabolcsi, Bence 89, 91, 206, 240
Szávai, Magda 185
Székely, Zoltán 92
Székelyhidy, Ferenc 121
Szekfű, Gyula 31
Szelényi, István 90, 166, 236
Széll, Jenő 178
Szent-Györgyi, Albert 161
Szigeti, József 246
Szigeti, Mihály 90, 166
Szolár, Ferenc 31
Szőke (?) 31
Szőnyi, Erzsébet 282
Sztojanovits, Adrienne 267
Tátrai, Vilmos 206
Telmányi, Emil 210
Temesváry, János 48
Toradze, David A. 248
Toscanini, Arturo 105, 106
Tóth, Aladár 88, 112, 162, 228, 240
Tóth, Margit 259

Török, Erzsébet 199
Tsintsadze, Sulkhan F. 248
Tulbure, György 31
Unger, Ernő 162
Vankó, Mrs. Juli Dudás 260
Várbíró, Judit 255
Vásárhelyi, Zoltán 112, 128, 187, 254
Vass (?) 31
Vékony Buri, Rudolf 215
Veres, Péter 165
Vermes, István 178
Vikár, László 184, 211
Vikár, Sándor 128, 134
Viski, János 214
Voinovich, Géza 165
Waldbauer, Imre 48
Walters, Gwendolyn 271
Willmetz (?) 156
Zathureczky, Ede 162, 171, 185
Zemplén, Géza 31
Zsadon, Andrea 255